BBQ
JOINTS

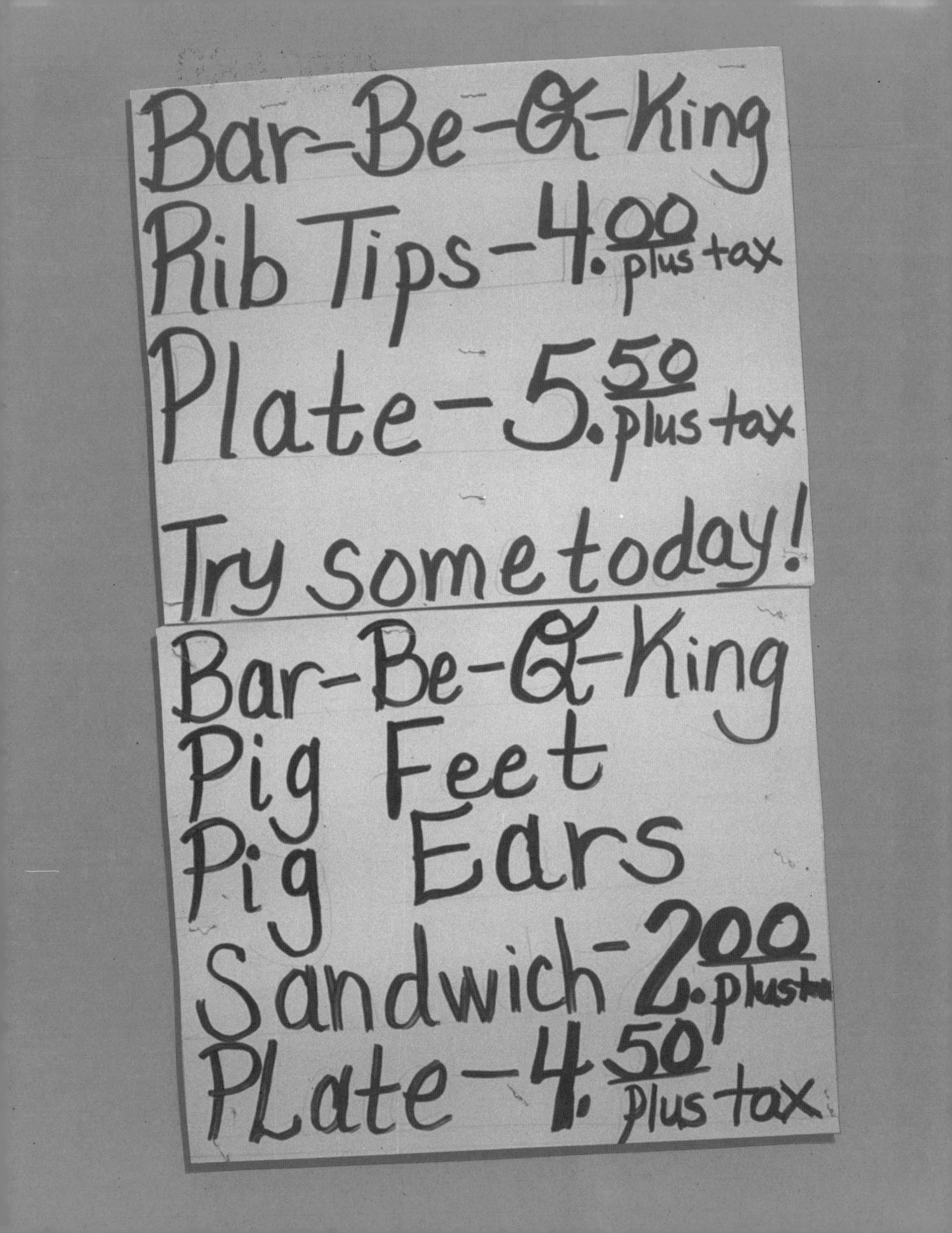

Bar-Be-Q-King

Rib Tips - 4.00 plus tax

Plate - 5.50 plus tax

Try some today!

Bar-Be-Q-King

Pig Feet

Pig Ears

Sandwich - 2.00 plus tax

Plate - 4.50 plus tax

BBQ JOINTS

STORIES AND SECRET RECIPES FROM THE BARBEQUE BELT

DAVID HOWARD GELIN

Gibbs Smith, Publisher
TO ENRICH AND INSPIRE HUMANKIND
Salt Lake City | Charleston | Santa Fe | Santa Barbara

First Edition
12 11 10 09 08   5 4 3 2

Published by
Gibbs Smith, Publisher
P.O. Box 667
Layton, Utah 84041

Orders: 1.800.835.4993
www.gibbs-smith.com

Designed by Kurt Wahlner
Printed and bound in Canada

Library of Congress Cataloging-in-Publication Data
Gelin, David Howard.
  BBQ joints : stories and secret recipes from the
barbeque belt / David Howard Gelin. — 1st ed.
      p. cm.
  ISBN-13: 978-1-4236-0218-7
  ISBN-10: 1-4236-0218-8
  1. Barbecue cookery—Southern States. 2.
Restaurants—Southern States—Guidebooks. I. Title.

TX840.B3G3945 2008
641.7'60975—dc22
                          2007041158

To my mom and dad

Contents

Acknowledgments

Buddy and I would like to single out Hamlin Endicott, Harvey Rubin, Barrett Batson and Candice Dyer. Without their advice and encouragement, this piece of work would never have been realized. Their acts, though seemingly small, have made all the difference in helping us get over the top.

Ray Lampe and John T. Edge, who I am now proud to call colleagues.

Buddy would like to single out Laura Dobson, Anja Tigges, Mitzi Cartee and Eric Mills for taking him in when it was just too hot to hang out in an unair-conditioned pickup truck.

Not in any particular order or function: J. Bradley Deal, Sheral Frohberg, Tim Springfield, John Donham, Scott Coleman, the Young family (homes in Texas and North Carolina), The Littwitz Family, Ken Lambert, Jack Fisher, Laurie Connor Jarrett, Mike and Jennifer Morrison, Mark Greenberg, Casey Coyne, Francis Parks, Nancy Bolling, Mitchell and Roni Moskowitz, Sadler Taylor, Stan Woodward, Walt Rogers, and all those wonderful librarians in towns big and small who didn't need to reference anything to steer me to the best barbecue around.

The good folks at Gibbs Smith, Publisher, not the least of which are Gibbs Smith, Pete Wyrick, Suzanne Taylor, Melissa Barlow, Kurt Wahlner, Jessica McKenzie, Renee Wald and Madge Baird.

My wonderful family who makes everything possible. My sisters (in chronological order) Beth, Deborah, Rachel and Martha. And especially my parents, Jack and Margaret, who would hope against incredible odds that their idiot son would someday find himself, which he did, somewhere on the open road between the pages of this book.

—David and Buddy

Barbecue has long been among the South's most democratic foods, cooked and served (and eaten) by all classes and hues. Today, that democracy is in flux. Once a working man's or woman's vocation, once a trade in which the underclass defined success, nowadays barbecue is often portrayed (and practiced) as a middle class avocation.

Increasingly, excellence is not measured by dedicated local customers who, through their patronage, pay homage to a neighbor's life of work in the pits. Part of the blame lies with the popularity of the barbecue competition circuits, where weekend warriors deem success to be a three-foot trophy bedecked with a plastic hog, presented on a bunting-draped stage by a lapsed Hooters girl, who, in advance of crowning the grand champion, shoehorned into a slinky sow costume and bobby pinned a pink-eared tiara to her hair.

David Gelin's *BBQ Joints: Stories and Secret Recipes from the Barbeque Belt* serves as a gentle corrective to this trend. Herein you meet the personalities behind the pits. You hear their family stories. Most important, you see their faces, creased by smiles full of pride in self, pride in place, and pride in tradition.

You might not agree with all of Gelin's subject choices, or even his geographical definitions of the American South. Based upon my own internal barometer of barbecue taste, Gelin and I are in accord sixty percent of the time. But a consensus of excellence is not this author's intent. He aims instead for a family portrait of Southern barbecue, and he delivers as much.

Thumb the pages that follow. Meet Susie Headrick, whose late husband Leo, of Leo and Susie's Famous Green Top Bar-B-Que in Dora, Alabama, was famous for singing along with the jukebox while using a hot sauce bottle as a microphone. Come face-to-face with Coleman Anderson of A&B Bar-B-Q in Jasper, Florida, who tells a tale of community fidelity when he says, "I don't buy firewood. It just shows up." Look closely and you will recognize a South where barbecue is a kind of national dish and the people who cook and serve it are, well, national heroes.

—John T. Edge
Author of *Southern Belly: The Ultimate Food Lover's Companion to the South*

WITH SO MANY WAYS TO SPELL IT, INCONSISTENCY JUST COMES WITH THE TERRITORY . . .

Only the truly mediocre are always at their best, and that certainly applies to barbecue. After all, barbecue is an art, not a science. I'm sure that even Michelangelo was not cranking out Davids every day. Heck, even Willie Nelson spewed out "To All The Girls I've Loved Before." It was probably said best by the seemingly invincible Hall of Fame pitcher Jim "Catfish" Hunter after he lost a World Series game: "The sun don't shine on the same dog's ass every day."

Barbecue is not a pretentious food. "The more simpler the better." Basically, it is meat slow-cooked over hardwood coals for hours. It is that simple. Different places have their own variations on that theme, but if you don't have those essential elements, you don't have barbecue. Or as Pete Jones put it, "If it's not cooked with wood, it's not barbecue."

That might seem obvious, but you would be surprised at what some try to pass off as barbecue. As in any art form, there are no rules, but there are a couple of red flags that you should be aware of:

- Chains are to be avoided—for so many, many reasons—at all cost. Stick with their burgers and extreme fajitas. Never, under any circumstances, order their ribs. They are most definitely grilled over gas and doused with some overly sweet, nasty sauce.

- The word *barbecue,* or some derivation thereof, should appear in the name of the joint. That is not to say that they can't serve other things, but the shorter the menu the better. That said, never order barbecue from a place that has an extensive menu, which by the way, includes barbecue. Especially if they give it a cutesy name like "riblets."

- One thing that's a lead-pipe-cinch is the bread. We are not talking the finest crusty, whole grain wheat that you have to eat now because it will be stale in an hour. Quite the contrary. We are talking bleached white, void of flavor, chemically altered to last an ice age or two. After all, it is that spongy quality that is perfect for sopping up barbecue sauce.

Which brings us to . . .

BLACK'S BBQ EST. 1932 TEXAS OLDEST AND BEST MAJOR BBQ RESTAURANT CONTINUOSLY OWNED BY THE SAME FAMILY

• Sauces are not necessary if the meat is cooked right. They should be used sparingly, preferably on the side. If a place drenches its ribs and 'cue in sauce there is probably a very good reason. If by chance they serve up generous portions drenched in barbecue sauce on a crusty Kaiser roll, GET OUT. Get out fast. If you get caught by an officer of the law for running out on your tab or for various other traffic infractions, simply explain the situation. Not only will he let you off, but he will probably offer a high-speed escort, with lights flashing and sirens blaring, to a worthy establishment.

• Moist towelettes—*pulleese!* That's what sleeves and paper towels are for.

• People in animal suits? Just wave as you drive by.

LuLu Roman

It's a good bet if . . .

- The joint is given a person's name, first or last (though nicknames are a plus) followed by some derivation of the word *barbecue*. Not only that, but one should be able to find that person at the joint during business hours. The name should not be that of a fictitious character (see "Chains" page 10). Incidental misspellings or bad grammar on signage or menus: a very good thing. Purposeful misspellings or bad grammar on signage or menus: a very bad thing.

It don't mean a thing . . .

- My apologies to the crooner who coined that famous phrase, but just because a place has plenty of statues (I dare say statuettes) of pigs or cows does not assure great barbecue. It doesn't necessarily mean bad barbecue, but I do personally believe that there is a point of diminishing returns.
- Jesus portraits (Bear Bryant in Alabama and Willie Nelson in Texas) and religious scripture do not always translate into heavenly barbecue, but I must say that the only time I was threatened with physical violence during the production of this book was when I was taking the picture of a joint with a sign that read "Jesus Saves."
- Another staple of barbecue decor is Old Glory. It appears most often in the classic flag form, but also in bunting, stickers, etc. Many places proudly proclaim "American Owned and Operated" just in case you didn't notice the twelve incarnations of Betsy Ross' handiwork.

13

CHURCH

There are no sacred cows (or pigs for that matter). That is why church and 'cue go so well together, though I will not vouch for the quality of the 'cue at these functions. Many churches have a pit, but all too often they are manned by a congregation member who doesn't know a pit from a hole in the ground.

Often they are catered by a worthy joint, so it's a crapshoot. But that is not the point. You are giving to the church and to the community which it serves, and even with mediocre 'cue, it is usually a wonderful experience. Go get yourself a plateful and some sweet tea. Mingle with the good folk. They don't call it soul food for nothing.

AND STATE

Along with a chicken in every pot, you can be assured of a heaping helping of bull and pork. If candidates want to appeal to the proletariat, they had better be prepared to chow down a lot of 'cue and kiss a lot of babies. I heard of a candidate in Texas who was in a heated campaign when he quipped that he was

looking forward to the end of the campaign because he was sick of barbecue. You can stick a fork in those political aspirations. He's done!

COOK-OFFS

These are primarily the domain of serious amateurs, but a few pros enter. As far as I can tell, their motivation is strictly bragging rights, highly sought in the barbecue world. The good folks who pursue these competitions put themselves through Hell for a little money, an enormous trophy and the chance to go to the granddaddies: Memphis in May, Jack

Daniel's World Championship, American Royal Barbecue, or the Houston Livestock Show and Rodeo.

My problem with these extravaganzas is that the presentation exceeds the actual craft. It has got to the point where Earl and his buddies need set designers and corporate sponsors to compete.

That said, cook-offs are a blast to attend. You can get a real appreciation for what goes into the preparation of great 'cue. Unfortunately, they can't sell you their wares (for health code reasons), but if you hang out until after the judging

(Saturday night) the party really takes off and they will literally throw the 'cue at you.

MAKING THE GRADE

It is not just about the 'cue, though every place in this book has worthy barbecue. However, most of the places that I visited *did not* make the cut.

I have many ways of finding places, from books, magazines and "best of" lists to just showing up and asking folks at filling stations. Police officers and firemen are excellent sources, but the very best source is a reference from a worthy barbecue peer. I always ask in closing, "With whom would you want to be associated?"

Sometimes they draw a blank, because they just don't get around. When they do give me a lead they are usually dead-on correct, and

when I tell the owners who sent me, they gush with pride.

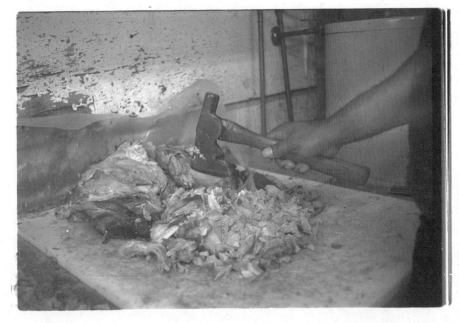

Because this is strictly subjective, and must pass through a committee of one, perhaps it is easier to state how a place *does not* make this book. That is easy: have lousy barbecue. A place might have the world's finest potato salad, but that can never make up for bad barbecue. I can, however, gladly recommend a place with great barbecue and lousy (store-bought) potato salad. I can't begin to tell you how many places I have been to that were everything I could ever hope for in a picture, and I could just tell that there was a gem of a story behind the place. But I couldn't be true to you if I steered you to a place where the food is just mediocre. I would leave with tears in my eyes and my credibility intact.

Another way to not make the cut is rudeness. I will never send anyone to a place where I feel they might be treated badly. This was extremely rare, but it did happen. I do not equate rude behavior with surliness. Many, many of these places have surly people running and working there, but asking someone to make serious barbecue and be a happy, humble host or hostess is asking a lot. I'll gladly accept great barbecue even if it is served with a scowl. I have also found that behind that gruff exterior can be a real heart of gold. If you want overly excited service, the chains are your best bet. They are trained to be that way.

About the only other surefire way not to make it in this book is to be overly cocky. "If you can do it then it ain't braggin,'" I heard "Dandy" Don Meredith once say, but I don't like it, and it is my book. I showed up at a place that was pleasant enough (I would not call it a joint). The 'cue was passable; not nearly the best, but far from the worst. The story of the owners was well documented and certainly interesting enough, but when I asked the question, "Whose place do you respect and admire and with whom would you like to be associated?" He responded, "I've been everywhere and I've tried everything, and there's nobody out there as good as me."

"Well, thank you very much for your time," I said and I beat a hasty retreat. For all I care, he has achieved legendary status in his mind and he can be featured in his own Hall of Fame all by himself. God bless him.

Well, Mr. Bovine Breath, how does a place actually make the cut then?

This book is by no means an objective attempt to answer any arguments about which is "the best" barbecue joint. I did not order any barbecue and dash off to my laboratory and examine it under a microscope. However, I have seen a "best of" list where they actually used a caliper to measure the depth of the smoke ring on the outside of a brisket.

In fact, I make a conscious effort *not* to talk about the food, unless there is something truly unique, like cassava with garlic sauce, strawberry-banana cake, or "brother-in-law." But if some joint's 'cue is not up to snuff, it will not appear in this book.

When I approach a promising joint, I survey the exterior. The funkier, the better. A lot of places would get a quick strike against them there, but I never rule them out on that alone. The old adage, "You can't judge a book unless you walk around in its shoes," or something

"BEST WAY"

THE BEST
WAY TO
FIND OUT
SOMEONE'S
WEALTH IS
BY THE
SMILE
THEY
WEARE.

Dan Segass

like that, certainly applies to barbecue joints.

Once inside the joint, I get an even stronger vibe. All my senses start going off. How does this place smell? What kind of music is being played? (I was at a famous joint and Kenny G was piped in. See ya!) What does the clientele look like? Do the folks working here look as if they've been here for decades?

If the answer is negative across the board, I might order a sandwich, just to confirm my intuition and if I'm hungry. Usually that sandwich is nothing to brag about. If I'm not hungry, I get a big cup of tea to go, and I'm on my way.

The best places have the feel of entering a small country church where the congregation has known each other their entire lives, where you are immediately recognized as a stranger, but given a real welcome: "What's your name?", "Where you from?", "What brings you 'round these parts?" and "The cobbler's real good today."

When you do stumble across one of these places, just let them bring it on. If you are fortunate enough you might get there at an off hour and get a seat at the counter next to a regular who introduces himself, joins in the praise and includes you in the conversation. After you enjoy a wonderful meal and polish off that last bite of cobbler, your stomach full and your soul fulfilled, you leave with a send-off and an invitation to come back real soon, knowing that the next time you will not be a stranger.

If you think that such places only exist in the movies, or in your grandparents' memories, you are dead wrong. They not only exist between the covers of this book, but they are out there. I hope that this book inspires you to visit one of these places or find one close to home. They are precious, and they need to be celebrated. They are like a hundred-year-old oak tree with roots in the community, one that has seemingly always been there and is just taken for granted. That is, until it's gone.

I'm not saying that every joint in here fits that description, but many do. Some of these places are as simple as a take-out window in a neighborhood, or a vegetable stand. Some are homes that are converted into barbecue joints and, yes, some are even part of a church.

This book is not just about the joints, but about the good folks who are the heart and soul of them. The owners, or "caretakers," as Reverend Richard Street calls himself, and their stories.

Many are born into it; many are called to it, and many, many more just sort of fell into it, but they all are interesting stories that will inspire you to do your best in whatever you do, no matter how humble, or at least inspire you to go out and get some 'cue.

Enjoy,

David Howard Gelin

"JUST FIRE AND HICKORY, BRICK AND SMOKE. DON'T SPICE UP NOTHIN,'"

George Archibald Jr. tells me as he hoses down the coals.

I'm sitting at the counter on one of the seven stools. On a nice day, you might want to eat outside. There are three picnic tables under the pines. Otherwise, you're getting it to go.

George Sr. started selling barbecue in this small building behind his home back in 1961. George Jr. remembers mopping the floors for a quarter a day back then.

George Jr. is joined behind the counter by his friend Arthur Wilkes. "We're a lot closer than

brothers; we're friends," says George. "We're both Juniors, and our fathers were friends. We used to be built for speed, but now we're built for comfort."

"That's *not* entirely true," a customer at the counter says. "You ought to see them at lunch time. People are lined up around this place and they're moving pretty good chopping ribs, making sandwiches, taking money."

At least they don't have to move very far. The pit is behind a sliding steel door, a couple of feet behind the counter, and they chop and slice the meat on a well-worn hickory block in front of the pit. In fact, everything at Archibald's is well worn: the driveway/parking lot, the counter, the floor, the stools, the steel door to the pit. Well-worn, but not worn out.

The sauce is truly legendary. It's the same recipe Betty Archibald concocted when they first opened up. In fact, while I was there, a guy who grew up in nearby Tuscaloosa and now resides in L.A. (Los Angeles, not Lower Alabama) was picking up six gallons. "I have barbecues all the time at my house," he said. "People are always asking about this sauce. I told them this is where I get it because they don't ship.

Somebody stole the last couple of jugs I had. You can rest assured that I won't be laying these ones out unguarded."

"I WANNA COOK CHICKEN JUST LIKE MY DADDY."

That is what Andrew Gibson Lilly told his kindergarten teacher when asked what he wanted to do when he grew up.

"Andrew 'Big Bob' Gibson, as he calls himself, has a way to go," chuckle his grandparents Don and Carolyn McLemore. "But we're confident he'll make it."

His nine-year-old sister, Caroline, does not want to work for her brothers. Grandma and Grandpa have encouraged her not to give up on the family business so soon. "They might end up working for you," they tell her.

The name Gibson is synonymous with barbecue in North Alabama. There are several descendants carrying on the family tradition. They all can trace their roots to "Big Bob's" backyard in 1925, where he tinkered with smoking hogs over an open pit. He's also been credited as the inventor of the famous "white sauce" that permeates Northern Alabama.

This particular branch of the Gibson barbecue family tree is now run by grandson Don McLemore, whose wife Carolyn is right there with him. To say they've known each other their entire lives would be an understatement. "My grandparents lived across from his grandparents. When I was born my mother tried to buy his stroller from

his mother, but they wouldn't sell. Don had a sister on the way."

Don always knew he was going to join the family business, which he did after Big Bob passed in 1972. Prior to that, he put in thirteen years as an accountant for the Burroughs Corporation.

Big Bob's would never be mistaken for a joint. It is a serious barbecue restaurant with the look and feel that says "bring the whole family." They also take cook-offs very seriously; more often than not walking away with top honors at Memphis in May.

These days, much of the day-to-day operation is handled by son-in-law Chris Lilly, who has recently been signed to host the *BBQ Championship Series* for the OLN network. That is, when he is not looking over his shoulder, the pitter-patter of footsteps he's hearing just might be someone gaining on him.

NOT QUITE BIG BOB GIBSON'S
WORLD–FAMOUS
NORTH ALABAMA
WHITE SAUCE

This goes especially well with chicken.

1 cup mayonnaise

1/2 cup lemon juice

3 ounces white vinegar

1 tablespoon sugar

1 tablespoon kosher salt

2 teaspoons coarse ground black pepper

Combine all ingredients in a bowl. Mix well and refrigerate for at least 1 hour. Store in a sealed container. It can last a good month. Makes about 2 cups.

DRIVE-THRU

HOME OF WORLD CHAMPIONSHIP BBQ

"ELVIS ATE HERE."

That's what James Taylor was told when he bought the place.

"I'm the third owner and he apparently had a horse farm not far from here. That was a long time ago. There haven't been any recent sightings."

James, a trained chef, was sent to work at a local country club when he decided to get a place of his own. He had enough moving around. It was time to put down roots.

"I grew up in West Virginia and Pennsylvania. I was a senior in high school living three miles from Three Mile Island when it had the near melt-down. My sister was away at college, and my parents were out of town. I was home alone. People were leaving and the National Guard was called in to prevent looting. It was *Twilight Zone* eerie. I remember hanging out and drinking beer with some of the guardsmen."

James is a music lover and guitar player. Blues and classic country are his tastes. There is a side patio at the joint where he and other musicians can gig. Jennifer began showing up more and more frequently. She started working at Big Cove and after a couple of years, she and James were married.

"I knew exactly what I was getting into. I married a man *and* a barbecue joint," she says from behind the order window.

The only water that I could see in the aptly named "Big Cove" is that tidal wave of urban sprawl coming from Huntsville, just over the mountain pass. Their humble little joint has literally been engulfed by Wal-Mart, Lowe's, Taco Bell and Kentucky Fried Chicken—not to mention many new homes. Business is better than ever, but how much longer can a little country joint survive as its natural habitat is encroached upon?

It makes sense that the Taylors are into preservation. They are very

active in The Music Maker's Relief Foundation, an organization that helps old blues musicians who have fallen on hard times.

"That sounds ironic, a blues musician fallen on hard times, but it is a shame to see these wonderful artists in such desperate circumstances. We find them, feed them, get them medical attention and shelter. If they want to, or can, perform, we find them gigs. They are always welcome here," James says.

Daniel, the Taylors' son, helps out and is also a musician—a drummer. "I want to go into the music business. Maybe start my own label or studio. I don't want to own this place!"

"He's still young. He'll be back in a couple decades," James adds.

"MOM WAS DEFINITELY THE BUSINESS SIDE. DAD WOULD HAVE BEEN HAPPY MAKING GREAT BARBECUE AND GOING BROKE,"

Van Sykes reveals to me. He is certainly his parents' child. Born into the business, he has been there and done that.

His father was a bread-truck driver whose barbecue roots can be traced back over a hundred years to the hills of Tennessee. His mother, Maxine, wanted to go into a business that they could do together, so they traded in their '54 Ford for a one-year lease on the original Bob Sykes Drive-In. They were successful, but didn't like the drive-in business, so they sold it and dad went to work as a manager of the first Kentucky Fried Chicken in Alabama. He would report directly to Harlan Sanders.

"He left after a couple of years to do for barbecue what the Colonel did for fried chicken," says Van. A lot of his bread-truck buddies became Bob Sykes franchise owners. "We had fourteen stores when we decided to pull the plug. Many of them are still around, but they are not under the 'Bob Sykes' name."

Van set up an operation to sell barbecue through Piggly Wiggly grocery stores. "I set it up, and it was going real well, but it was not for me."

Van ended up selling it to a well known barbecue chain. That experience has only reinforced his belief that barbecue is best when it is fresh. "I try to manage the flow as if we are on the verge of running out." Not an easy proposition when it takes eight to twelve hours to make great barbecue.

Even though Van is concentrating on his one and only store, he will gladly share his lifetime of expertise with anyone wishing to join the ranks of owner/operator of a barbecue restaurant—as a paid consultant.

He will help you design your restaurant. Get you going on your way to success.

Money well spent.

VAN SYKES'S CLASSIC ONION RINGS

3 jumbo yellow onions

1-1/2 cups whole milk

3 large eggs

3/4 teaspoon salt

1-1/2 cups self-rising flour

oil (canola or peanut)

Slice onions into 1/2-inch rings. Whisk milk, eggs and salt. Gradually add flour until batter is smooth. Dip onion slices.

Heat oil to 375 degrees in either a fryer or in a frying pan and fry onion slices until golden brown. Remove and place on paper towels to cool.

"IF LOSING YOUR CUSTOMERS AND MOST OF YOUR MONEY DOESN'T SHAKE YOUR FAITH, THEN NOTHING WILL,"

Bill Armbrecht tells me from the dining room, where every inch of the wall and ceiling has an accolade, either published or handwritten. "They were working on the road that runs by my place, making it very difficult for my customers to get in and out of here. The project had been dragging on for well over a year with seemingly no end in sight. Things were looking real bleak. That's when I told myself, 'If God is trying to tell me that he wants me to do something else, then I'll gladly accept that and quit worrying.'"

Coincidentally (or not), the roadwork kicked into a higher gear, and within a couple of weeks the project was complete—just in time for the big Fourth of July weekend. Hallelujah!

Before running The Brick Pit, Bill considered going into law, like his father. "But after two years of college my heart just wasn't in it," he says. "I always enjoyed sailing. That's all I wanted to do, so I joined a yacht crew and eventually worked my way up to captain and sailed boats up and down the eastern seaboard for twelve years.

When Bill met Susan, she joined his crew and eventually became first mate, in more ways than one: before long, the two were married. Eventually they decided to return to dry land and came back to settle in their hometown of Mobile.

"I bought interest in a temporary business," Bill says. "It was pretty good, but it wasn't for me. I ended up selling my share and said to myself,

'What do *you* want to do?' Since I was a kid I've enjoyed making barbecue. And when your name is Armbrecht and people have been calling you 'Brick' your whole life, you can say the seeds for a place called 'The Brick Pit' have long been sown. Susan understood. She was supportive and very helpful in getting The Brick Pit off the ground."

Now that the road is fixed, folks have been wearing it out to sample Bill's 'cue, which is legendary for its extra-slow smoking process, the times of which are proudly posted at the ordering window.

"I have been fortunate enough to make a lot of 'Best of' lists," Bill says, "but my all-time favorite recommendation was when Franklin Graham testified about my ribs on stage during his crusade."

Pass the barbecue sauce.

FROM BILL ARMBRECHT OF THE BRICK PIT, A TIP FOR BUYING MEAT

Unfortunately, the meat we get at the local grocery store is not always of the best quality. This is especially true when it comes to ribs. The grocery-store ribs tend to be too lean, not meaty enough. Bill recommends finding a local meat distributor. They cater to restaurants, but many have a small shop that sells to the general public. Distributors can be found in the Yellow Pages under "Meat." Bill suggests calling in advance, just to make sure that you can buy from them. When buying ribs, you should ask for "3-1/2 down." This cut includes some of the meaty shoulder section. It doesn't dry out and can take low, slow cooking.

"HE ONLY MADE TWO GOOD DECISIONS HIS WHOLE LIFE,"

says Susie Headrick. "The other was marrying me."

"When he told me he was going to buy the Green Top back in '71, I would have no part of it, but he did it anyway." Back then, the Green Top was more bar than barbecue. A place where the locals could let off a little steam after their shift in the coal mine. "It did make sense that he own it, but I really just thought it was an excuse to fuel his drinking."

The previous owner, Edith Carey, had so much confidence in Leo that she viewed the sale as a paid vacation. Thinking Leo would fall flat on his face, she would get the Green Top back at a fire-sale price.

Being a business owner did not change Leo one iota. He was the same good timing guy as before. "If it wasn't for my dad and uncle, we never would have made it," grandson and now manager Tony Headrick told me. "They both left the mines to run the place and grandpa was the entertainment. He would sing to the customers using a Crystal Hot Sauce jar as a microphone.

People would come just to see him. We even |had some 'Lovable Leo' T-shirts printed up. I still hear stories about people wearing their shirt on vacation half way around the world and someone recognizing it."

The Green Top did eventually win over Susie, and it was under her management that the transition from rowdy roadside bar

to family-friendly barbecue joint took place. "We sell a lot more tea than beer now. A lot more," Tony says. That change did not occur overnight.

Back in the day, Susie used to keep a night stick behind the counter and was not afraid to brandish it to straighten out a miner who may have had a few too many. That crowd now goes to Welsey's Booby Trap down across the road.

NOT ON THE MENU
"HOPPIN'" JOHN

1/2 pound bacon

2 cloves garlic

1 medium yellow onion

1 pound dry black-eyed peas

Fry up the bacon in a skillet. Drain grease and chop up bacon. In the now greasy skillet, stir in the garlic and onion. Wash beans.

In a pot with 6 cups water, cook the dry black-eyed peas (do not soak overnight). Bring to a boil and reduce to a simmer. Combine with cooked bacon, onion and garlic. Stir occasionally and cook with lid on for about 1-1/2 hours, or until beans are tender. Do not over cook. Serve with equal amount of rice.

"I AM THIS PLACE. AND THIS PLACE IS ME,"

says John Strickland.

"I came back here to visit my parents. My dad was in real bad shape, so I decided to stay. I found this log home that was also zoned commercial. Me and my brother dismantled it and put it back together, converting it into a barbecue joint."

John Strickland was from Florala, a town named for its location right on the Florida border on the Alabama side. His life has been an amazing journey that has brought him full circle.

"NEVER GIVE UP"

After graduating from Florala High, John enlisted in the air force. He spent a couple of years in Vietnam. Once back, John picked a very safe career, dietetics, which he studied at the University of Southern Mississippi.

"I was all set for a quiet career. I went to work for Morrison's Cafeteria. They sent me to Houston to be an assistant manager at a hospital where they had a food-service contract. I was hired by a relative of the Morrison family, and whenever he came to visit, he always asked about the family, which he knew by name. Back then they did everything from scratch, and nothing went to waste. That was perfect training for a career in food service."

With a solid foundation, John was equipped to do just about anything in food service. His experiences varied from being a cook off the Louisiana coast on an oil rig, to starting up an upscale steak and seafood restaurant chain that was housed in railroad boxcars; from being an executive chef in a luxury hotel in Houston to running the entire food and housing services for the three largest construction camps in the world in Saudi Arabia.

"All of the places had their own unique challenges. I always enjoyed meeting them," John says with satisfaction.

John even left food service on a couple of occasions. In fact, at the time he went to visit his parents, he was a tax collector in the Alaskan bush country.

"All the while I loved Texas barbecue, but even with all my culinary knowledge, I couldn't make a good brisket. One day I stopped by this roadhouse in Mesquite, Texas. The place was a dump, but it had the best brisket I ever had. I asked the guy working there how he done it. He showed me and I've been doing it that way ever since."

"This is most definitely a barbecue joint, but I only serve healthy food. There is an obesity epidemic going on. People are eating too much refined flours and sugars. I refuse to serve fried foods.

"People see this big star on the floor, the Texas-style barbecue, and the Starlight Grill and think I named it after Texas, but that's not the case. There used to be a Starlight Drive-In here when I was a kid. That was my favorite place growing up."

BRISKET DONE RIGHT ACCORDING TO
JOHN STRICKLAND OF STARLIGHT GRILL

This is a very time consuming process, but well worth the effort.

Use a fresh whole brisket that is about 12 to 14 pounds. Place in a 3-inch-deep pan (big enough to hold). Inject with favorite injector marinade (John recommends Dale's). Give it a good coating of garlic powder (not garlic salt). Cover with plastic wrap and then foil and set overnight in fridge.

Early morning, put the brisket on the smoker at 200 to 225 degrees for 10 to 12 hours. Do not throw out the marinade or wash the marinade pan. You will put the brisket back in the pan after smoking. Put smoked brisket into the fridge overnight again.

Before time to serve, put the panned brisket (do not remove cover) in a 250-degree oven for about 4 hours.

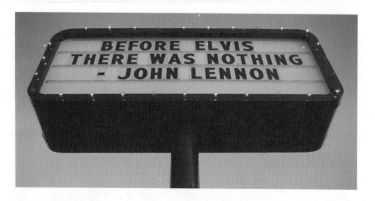

ELVIS'S POUND CAKE
(SUBMITTED BY JOHN STRICKLAND)

John says, "This recipe was developed by his next door neighbor in Tupelo, Mississippi, where he grew up. I got the recipe from her at a food show in Houston. It was later published in the *Houston Chronicle*. She would send one of these cakes to Graceland about every month."

3 sticks butter

3 cups sugar

8 ounces heavy whipping cream

2 tablespoons vanilla extract (use the real stuff, no imitation)

1 teaspoon lemon extract

3 cups flour (Swan's Down cake flour)

8 large eggs

1/2 teaspoon salt

Preheat oven to 325 degrees.

Cream together butter, sugar and whipping cream. Add vanilla and lemon extract. Add the flour, eggs and salt. Beat this batter for 10 minutes or more, until the batter seems to lighten in color. What is happening with color change is the incorporation of air. Bake for 1-1/2 hours.

"I DIDN'T NEED TO THINK TWICE ABOUT WHAT TO DO WHEN THE DOCTOR TOLD ME I COULDN'T BE A DIESEL MECHANIC ANYMORE,"

Jim Vaughan tells me as he is showing off the newer, bigger smoker he made.

"That was the second time I tore up my back. It's been ten years since we've opened up this place." The other part of the "we" in J&N is wife Nora.

Jim was a serious hobbiest before he went at barbecue full time. In fact, when Clinton was governor, Jim went to Little Rock and cooked for the legislature. "The chickens were supplied by Tyson's. We supplied about a dozen raccoons."

When they first started out, they had a much better location. It was owned by a friend in the

construction business who Jim used to maintain trucks for. "When I asked him about putting a trailer on his land, he told me I was the only person he would let stay there." The road was eventually widened and so they had to move their trailer to its current location a little off the beaten path, but that's okay because the folks in the Jonesboro area know where to find them.

They still operate out of that trailer, but it has been expanded a couple of times. "I have a regular who works in the advertising business who wants me to run some ads. I told him I couldn't afford to do it. He keeps after me and I just had to tell him I couldn't handle all that business he was going to get me."

It's not that Jim doesn't take professional advice. In fact, he's building a snow-cone room at the urging of his fifteen-year-old granddaughter, Brook.

"Everything just fell right into place," Nora tells me.

"It has brought our family closer together because everyone helps out whenever they can. We even have a five-year-old great granddaughter, Emily. Whenever she's here, she clears off the picnic tables. That is the job that she gave herself. One time a customer gave her a dollar tip. She always talks about it, and will never forget it.

JIM VAUGHAN'S BUDDY PAUL CALKIN'S COON BURGERS

1-1/2 ounces salt pork

1/2 medium yellow onion

1 (6-inch) stalk celery

1/2 teaspoon salt

1/2 teaspoon black pepper

1/8 teaspoon cayenne pepper

Trap a good-size raccoon. Clean and dress him. Put the meat through a meat grinder. For each pound of raccoon meat, add the above list of ingredients. Put through grinder again. Shape into desired-size patties and grill like hamburgers.

"I JUST HAD TO RE-OPEN THIS PLACE. THE RIGHT WAY,"

Ronald Settlers says as he leans back in his chair overlooking the dining area.

Ronald exudes authority. He's a man you do not cross. He watches me nibble on a plate of his "fall-off-the-bone" ribs.

"Where'd you learn to eat ribs!" he shouts. "You put the end in your mouth. Go ahead. It's all good.

"My great uncle and aunt, Allen and Amelia Sims, opened this place in '37. They sold fish and hamburgers, but it was mostly a beer and domino joint. That's the last of the domino tables from back then over by the door. They eventually started selling barbecue, and that's when this place really took off. Zoning didn't much exist. On this side of town you could pretty much get away with anything. Now, we are grandfathered in.

"They retired in '76 and didn't have any kids. My family looked to me to take over. I had a good job with Strickland Truck Lines. I worked the loading dock and drove local. I didn't want to take over this place.

"They leased the place to Economy Foods, who thought they could just take it over, so they had no need for the recipes or training. It got so bad that I finally just gave in to family and friends and took back control.

"When I re-opened, a few months later on October 2, people just flocked here. Having been involved with this place most of my life, I thought I could handle it, but the neighborhood response was just too much. I ended up quitting my truck job that December, a lot sooner than I wanted.

"Over the years, I expanded by opening up a

couple of other locations in town, but what I'd really like to do before I die, is put 'Sims on Wheels.' Outfit a semi truck and take it to big cities, ones with over 500,000 people. Use it as a marketing tool."

Ronald doesn't see himself retiring anytime soon. He has a son and daughter working here, but he says, "We'll cross that bridge when we come to it."

BRINE SOAKING MEATS
(THIS TECHNIQUE IS NOT USED AT SIM'S)

This technique is used primarily on wild game to help remove the "gamey" taste of venison and other strong meats. Brining works well with turkey and pork, but is not recommended for beef.

1 pound salt (sea salt or pickling salt that does not contain iodine)

3 gallons fresh cool water (use less or more, but maintain the ratio)*

Combine salt and water and make sure that the salt is completely dissolved. Add meat, making sure that all the meat is covered. If it is winter and the outside temperature is good and cool, you can put the brining meat outside; otherwise, put it in the refrigerator. Soak for at least 24 hours.

*It's best to allow chlorinated tap water to sit uncovered overnight. This will allow the chlorine to dissipate.

"TRUCKERS PUT US ON THE MAP."

I guess you would call it a little professional courtesy, since William and Cecelia Wood operate out of a Winnebago. Legend has spread over the CB radio about this barbecue stand carved out of a rice field on the corner of state Highways 14 and 49 in remote north-eastern Arkansas.

There may only be eighty people in town, but when the main Wal-Mart distribution center is fifty miles down the road, you are on one of the major truck routes in the country.

William fell into barbecuing to supplement his income back in 1985. He was a crop duster, which made him very busy during spring and fall, but not very busy during the rest of the year. "I thought of it as giving me a little extra fishing money. Now, I'm so busy I don't have time to go fishing, or crop dusting for that matter." He gave that up to devote himself full time to barbecuing in 1991. Cecelia has been riding shotgun from the start.

"You can really feel the weather out here," Cecelia tells me from her station in the Winnebago. Their stand is surrounded by flat rice fields for as far as the eye can see. "It has gotten in the single digits in winter and over a hundred during the summer," William adds as he checks the meat in the smoker. It is early spring, but he is already in mid-summer form, his fair skin already beet red. This is only emphasized by his snow white hair.

As humble as this little stand is, don't be fooled. They do move a lot of barbecue, but that is just the tip of the iceberg. "People were always asking to buy our sauces, so we started bottling them," Cecelia tells me as she makes a couple of sandwiches to go. When you start off by winning first places from the National Barbecue Association and the Dallas Gourmet Market, people take notice. William and Cecelia have expanded into marinades and dry rubs and the awards have kept coming. Today they are the sole wholesale distributors of their concoctions. Not bad for a little stand at the crossroads.

WOODY'S BARBECUED RICE

Grand Prize Winner: Riceland Rice Cook-Off

First place: Arkansas Rice Festival

2 cups rice, uncooked

4 cups chicken broth

1 clove garlic, minced

1 green bell pepper, diced

1 (14.5-ounce) can tomatoes and green chiles

8 green onions, thinly sliced

2 tablespoons Bar-B-Q dry rub (Preferably Woody's)

Combine ingredients in an aluminum drip pan and seal tightly with foil. Place on center rack and cook at 350 degrees until rice is done and liquid is absorbed (about 40 minutes). [All ingredients may be mixed together and cooked in rice cooker or on stovetop over medium heat.] Fluff and let set 5 minutes before serving.

"I HAD A PERFECT RECORD."

Coleman Anderson had logged over a million miles, accident-free. Then one day he was unloading his rig and threw his back out. "I hurt my back unloading groceries," he says shaking his head.

Coleman's home is on Route 41 in Jasper, Florida, right in the middle of town. "I just sat home and with the help of some friends built a barbecue pit in my front yard. We just hung out and barbecued all day. Deer, wild hog, rabbit, gator—you name it, we probably cooked it.

"One day the health inspector showed up and told us we couldn't sell meat without a license. Well, I wasn't selling it, and he told us we should. He helped me out every step of the way. Helped with all the paperwork, told me to put on a roof,

and a bathroom, helped me with the food management course. It took me a couple of times, but I passed it. It's been fifteen years and I've passed every inspection.

"Me and my buddies built this place. The bathroom was from a house that was being torn down. I don't buy firewood. It just shows up. One time the tree guy just dropped a huge pile. The logs were too big. I had to track him down to cut them smaller.

"The only time I ever came close to getting in any trouble was when the police took exception to my sign that read, 'If you bring it, we'll smoke it.' I added the word 'meat,' just so that nobody would get any wrong ideas," Coleman adds with a chuckle.

A&B doesn't have what you might call a "formal" dining area. What it does have is a majestic canopy of 150-year-old oak trees accented with Spanish moss hanging down. Just pull up a lawn chair or a log and enjoy.

A&B is a magnet for people. The locals stop by and make an afternoon of it. One guy was there mending the holes in his fishing net. He was not about to leave any time soon. Another stopped by to show off his new truck all assembled. All the while horns were constantly honking and people were waving. It would be rude to drive past and not acknowledge your friends and neighbors at A&B.

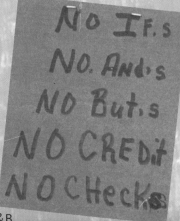

"I STARTED OUT IN THE MAIL ROOM,"

Billy Cowart tells me from a seat at a booth in his venerable joint.

That was in June of 1952, and the mailroom was at the Jacksonville Federal Reserve. By the time he left in 1967, he had risen to the position of Assistant Manager of Check Clearing. Billy left to strike out on his own selling insurance and preparing tax returns. A couple of years later, Billy was tapped to help start up a new Federal Reserve branch they were building in Miami.

"I got my old job back, but since I didn't have a college degree, that was as far as I could go. They gave the manager's position to a kid with a piece of paper, so it was back home to Jacksonville for me."

Billy resumed his tax business and started doing payroll for several small businesses around town. One of which was Fred Cotten's.

"Fred Cotten's has been a Jacksonville institution since 1948. When I was a kid in the '50s my softball team would meet here after games. Nobody called it Fred Cotten's. Everybody called it Lucille's, after Miss Lucille Baker, who ran the place.

"In the early '60s I hunted at a nearby hunting camp. Among my responsibilities included barbecuing the wild game. I would use Fred's Sauce.

"I also had food service experience from my time in the National Guard. I was appointed sergeant in charge of the mess hall, a position that nobody wanted, and it showed. I, however, looked at it as an opportunity to prove myself, and at next year's Annual Training, we were awarded 'Best Mess,' which led to the promotion of First Sergeant, and a few years later I was promoted to Sergeant Major of the one-hundred and eleventh Aviation Brigade.

"That experience really prepared me in running this operation. I was doing the taxes and payroll and dealing with Miss Lucille, who was still running this place after nearly fifty years as well as Mr. Cotten's widow, who was retired to Tennessee. She turned ownership over to her granddaughters, who really had no interest in running the place. I offered to buy the place from them, which I did in May of 2000.

"When I purchased this place, I was hoping

LARGE PORK OR BEEF SANDWICH $5.25

Lucille would stay on, but several weeks in, she decided to retire. Luckily for me Willie Willis, Janice Starks and Johnnie Brown had been on staff for many years and were more than capable of filling the void. They are the ones that keep this place going. I'm very fortunate they stayed on to help me."

JANICE STARKS OF FRED COTTEN'S TIP
FOR COOKING CORN ON THE GRILL

Place corn still in the husks on the grill. Make sure that the heat is low, about 250 to 300 degrees. Turn corn about every 15 minutes. After about 45 minutes on the grill, remove husks and place corn back on grill for another 30 minutes and then turn after about 15. After cooking, butter, salt and pepper to taste.

"It goes for the customers as well as my employees, and don't think that rule doesn't apply to family members, too," John Williams tells me. He should know. That sign could and probably should state, "I won't back down."

John has been a landscaper and a horse trainer, among other things, but he always had a love for barbecuing, even before he officially opened up his own barbecue shed in 2000.

"At first, it seemed the deck was stacked against me. I ran into all kinds of obstacles. In my first location, the health department kept changing the rules. First, I complied with the coding issues. Suddenly, I wasn't zoned for a barbecue establishment. Next, my 22-foot smoker blew out. Shortly thereafter, the smoker blew me out. I suffered second- and third-degree burns and had to be airlifted to the burn unit. It was speculated it could have been sabotaged. With the love of family and friends, I fully healed in two years. My injuries involved the use of my hand and I had a hole in my elbow. Whether a stumbling block or sabotage, the show must go on. My mom, Gertie, made me promise to relocate and continue my dream. With the financial backing from her and other family, Gertie's BBQ opened the week she passed away, at the age of eighty-nine.

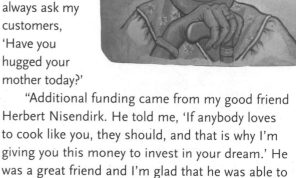

"Everybody who ever met my mother loved her. She was very personable. She also taught me how to cook. That is why I always ask my customers, 'Have you hugged your mother today?'

"Additional funding came from my good friend Herbert Nisendirk. He told me, 'If anybody loves to cook like you, they should, and that is why I'm giving you this money to invest in your dream.' He was a great friend and I'm glad that he was able to see this place succeed before he passed away in '05 at the age of ninety-two."

John and his family chose well. Their new location under a majestic oak and magnolia is a converted stone house. It is an apt setting for a family that will not be moved, whose business is rooted in love, family, friendship and the love of God.

GERTIE WILLIAM'S
"RECIPE FOR LIFE"

1 cup love for all mankind

$^1/_2$ cup patience for the most difficult customers

1 tablespoon forgiveness for the vendor who delivers late

1 teaspoon of "The Look" when the ribs are smokin'

2 cups grace for the unruly child

1 sliver of a smile to some a little out of sorts

4 dashes kindness to every boy, girl, woman and man
   you meet

Mix all the ingredients together. You will never meet a stranger. God's love will follow you wherever you go. People will forget why they were ever troubled. Your smile will light up the darkness. At the end of the day, you'll look in the mirror and know, there is a way. You can't put this recipe in a pot and cook it. You can't put it in a cookbook and let it sit. You can't go wrong because you forgot an ingredient. You can go forth and live the life. Loved by all, was our Gertie. Serves all mankind.

"I NEVER HAD BARBECUE BEFORE."

In Cuba, they do not have barbecue like we know it. It was only after Alfredo Rosales literally won the immigration lottery and was able to come to America that he was able to enjoy barbecue (and freedom).

"I had some ribs at Tony Roma's (a chain) and thought this was the most wonderful thing I've ever had. Then a friend brought me here. I've been coming back every day since."

In Cuba, Alfredo had the title of Animal System Engineer, a very responsible position for meat distribution on the island. Then, on August 3, 1995, he came to this country with his wife, Lissett, and daughter, Ana Isabel. They settled in the Little Havana district of Miami, where he went to work for an uncle who owned a Mr. Food convenience store.

Alfredo worked hard and saved his money. And spent his free time at Uncle Tom's Barbecue, his new home away from home in his new homeland.

Since 1948, Uncle Tom's has been the one constant in Little Havana, even before it was called Little Havana. Uncle Tom's has not abandoned its barbecue heritage, but has added a Cuban twist. You can get some 'cue with a side order of fried plantains, or cassava with garlic sauce.

"The barbecue has not changed one bit," a woman at the next table assured me as she

enjoyed a big plate of ribs. "I've been coming here since I was a little girl in the late 1950s."

Alfredo tells me, "I found out the owners wanted to sell the place. I could not let this opportunity pass. So with money I had saved from working for my uncle and a loan from the Terra Bank [The Commercial Bank of Nicaragua], I was able to get this place.

"This is the greatest country in the world. I am so happy to be here. You have the freedom to do anything you want," Alfredo says with pride.

"My daughter is in high school and she wants to be an artist or a graphic designer. That is okay with me. I think she should be able to do whatever she wants. She is 100 percent American."

Alfredo is generously sharing his good fortune and hard work with others. The latest is his cousin Eudaldo. Just four months ago, he too migrated from Cuba. He is seeing first-hand the bounty that this land has to offer (and the barbecue).

ALFREDO ROSALES'
UNCLE TOM'S
CASSAVA
WITH GARLIC SAUCE

Multiply ingredients by number of people to be served.

1 cassava (yuca)
2 tablespoons olive oil
2 cloves garlic, crushed
2 tablespoons lemon juice

Boil water in a pot big enough to accommodate however many cassavas (yucas) you will be preparing. Let them boil for a good 20 minutes, until soft.

Garlic Sauce: In a small frying pan on moderate heat, mix appropriate portions of olive oil, garlic and lemon juice. Mix together.

Cut open cassavas and pour sauce over top.

"I THOUGHT I COULD RUN A BARBECUE JOINT PART TIME,"

Simmie Nichols tells me. "That was a *big* mistake. I would call during the day and no one would answer the phone. When I did get ahold of the employees, they told me they needed to run to the store, or some other emergency. It just wasn't working out. I realized that I had to quit my job or close B-B-Q King."

Growing up in St. Augustine, Florida, Simmie worked at a small neighborhood supermarket with a quick-serve restaurant. He always enjoyed helping out and having the relationships with his neighbors, something that a barbecue joint offers.

Simmie came to Albany, Georgia, to attend Albany State University, where he earned degrees in biology and chemistry. To help pay for his education he worked for Trailways Bus Lines as a ticket agent. He also loaded and unloaded busses.

After graduation Simmie applied for jobs in the sciences.

"When I saw the salaries they were offering for research positions, I went right back to Trailways. I became a bus driver. I enjoyed the work, but after ten years on the road, my wife gave me an ultimatum. Either drive busses or start a family. That is when I went back to Albany State and got a job in their transportation department. I eventually rose to level of Director, in charge of the busses and all their fleet of vehicles.

"I always wanted a barbecue place, and in 1990 I went into business with Marvin Mills. We opened M&N Bar BQ House. He was under the impression that you just opened the door and the people and the money poured in. It doesn't quite work that way, so I ended up buying him out pretty early on and owning this place outright.

"I love owning a barbecue joint. It's not for everyone, but it's for me. I gave up a nice job with great benefits and security, but I don't regret it for a minute. I always get a kick when one of my customers recognizes me on the street and says, 'I'd really like a sandwich,' like I got some in my truck or back pocket."

SIMMIE NICHOLS' "B–B–Q KING"
PIG EAR SANDWICH

You can't make silk purses out of 'em, but they do make a tasty sandwich!

1 green bell pepper

1 yellow onion

6 pig ears

2 tablespoons Lawry's seasoned salt

2 tablespoons granulated garlic

2 tablespoons lemon pepper

Cut up bell pepper and onion and then place in an 8 x 12-inch aluminum pan with 3 cups water. Sprinkle in the rest of the ingredients. Put plastic wrap on top, followed by aluminum foil. Sit on grill at 375 degrees for 2 to 3 hours. They are done when a plastic fork or toothpick can go through an ear with ease. Serve on white bread, 1 ear per sandwich. Add barbecue sauce, mustard, and hot sauce to taste. You can also cook pig's feet the same way, but don't put them in a sandwich.

"KNOW THE LORD FIRST. PUT YOUR TRUST IN HIM."

"Prayer is the key to heaven. Faith unlocks the door. Make sure you got a lot of faith and forget about fishing for a while," Phillip Bass, aka Bubba, tells me as he tends to his chicken and butts over the pit.

"I came to barbecuing growing up in Columbus, Georgia, where folks eat more barbecue per capita than any other city in Georgia, maybe even the entire country. We had four barbecue joints on one block. My buddy Chuck Farrell's family owned The Smoky Pig just across the river in Phoenix City, Alabama. I would hang out there and help out. I wasn't on the payroll. I got paid in barbecue. I was in my early twenties and didn't consider it a job."

Bubba is a natural salesman. For a time, he worked as a route salesman of over-the-counter pharmaceuticals. He lasted seven years. It's a hard life on the road.

"Chuck opened up a place of his own, in Opekia, Alabama. I ended up going to work for him, and this time took it seriously. I learned that to make it in this business, great barbecue isn't enough. You got to have great sides and everything else."

It's a practice Bubba has put into good use at his establishments, first in Albany for thirteen years, then in Tifton, where he has been a favorite since 1991. "Our steak sandwich we have here isn't cheap steak. It's thinly sliced prime rib. Our cakes are baked daily, and are fourteen layers," Bubba proudly states.

"The best part of owning a barbecue joint is the people you come in contact with, be it your customers or employees. There is this family here in town that sponsored an exchange student for Japan. They were regulars here. For her last meal she said, 'How do you explain "Bubba" to people back in Japan?'

"I thought about it for a minute and said, 'Bubba is kinda like Buddha,' as I tapped my ample midsection."

"BUBBA" BASS'S TIP TO ENSURE GREAT BARBECUE

Use only on pork and chicken—not beef.

1/4 cup salt

1 lemon

Take an empty 2-liter plastic Coke® bottle; drill a 1/8-inch hole in the middle of the screw-on cap. Mix the salt and juice from the lemon in the Coke bottle; fill with warm water. Shake to dissolve the salt. During the slow cooking process, periodically sprinkle the meat with the lemony brine. It not only adds flavor, but regulates the temperature to ensure slow cooking.

PHILLIP "BUBBA" BASS'S TIP FOR COOKING A BEEF STEAK

Use only charcoal and get the grate as close to the charcoal as possible. Get the charcoal white hot. Put steak on grill. Turn almost immediately. Keep turning almost immediately until the steak is done to your preference. This should only take a few minutes. Using high heat and constant turning seers without burning, and locks in the meat's natural juices.

"I GOT FIRED MY FIRST DAY."

A dubious start indeed for Doug Fincher Jr. as he looks back on a lifetime of barbecue.

"I was about five or six and I didn't hang the tray right on the car door. The food ended up all over the customer. My dad sent me home, which was next door. I came back the next day and I never made that mistake again."

Fincher's Barbecue was started two times in 1935. The first effort was made by Doug Jr.'s grandfather, Arthur. He bought a stand, but after three months, it burned to the ground. His son Doug, or "Dude" as he was better known, reopened it on the same ground where the original Fincher's

Barbecue stands today, on Route 41. That used to be the main road to and from Florida, before I-75 was built. Arthur then reopened his own place on Columbus Road. It was taken over by Dude's brother, Raymond, and remained open until 2002.

Fincher's Barbecue has the unique distinction of being the "first barbecue in space." Space Shuttle astronaut Sonny Carter was a high school classmate of Doug Jr., as well as a huge fan. At a reunion, Doug jokingly mentioned, "Why don't you take some up there with you." Sonny said that he'd see what he could do.

Doug sent him a shoulder and some sauce and the NASA scientists freeze-dried it, giving new meaning to the term "take out."

Doug Jr. went to Georgia Southern in Statesboro for three years before he decided that barbecue was going to be his life.

His wife Alice, who was also his high school sweetheart, graduated from Georgia Southern, and was all set to embark on a career as a teacher, but she never made it to school.

"We were due to get married in October, and right after graduation, Doug's mother told me to

come over and help out. I've been here ever since."

That is a very believable story, since several non-family employees have worked for the Fincher's for over thirty years.

Doug III has followed in his father's footsteps. Having too much fun at the University of Georgia, he ended up finishing his business degree at nearby Mercer. After graduation, he started to work full time. Doug III is looking to expand the business beyond their four locations in and around Macon, and get their sauce in stores. Maybe he can establish the first barbecue joint on the moon.

FINCHER'S DEEP-FRIED SKINS

pork skins and oil

After the ham or shoulder has smoked for 8 to 12 hours scrape the fat.

In a deep fryer, heat the oil to 375 degrees.

Fry skins until they float or until they stop bubbling. Flip over and fry until that side no longer bubbles.

Remove from oil and let sit for 10 minutes. Skins will harden. Break up and eat.

"YOU CAN TELL A LOT ABOUT A PERSON BY SITTING ACROSS A TABLE AND LOOKING INTO THEIR EYES,"

Kenneth Melear tells you from behind his big oak desk just back of the cash register, unlit stogie hanging out the side of his mouth.

He ought to know. After all, he served as chief magistrate judge for 28 years, but that was only a part-time job. Except for a three-year stint in the army, he has been in the barbecue business his entire life.

"My grandfather started the first Melear's Barbecue before I was born. I don't remember exactly when. But you could get a bowl of stew for a nickel." That was in LaGrange. His father tried his hand as a cotton mill manager, but the lure of smoking shoulders was too much. He opened his own place in Union City in 1942. Kenneth learned the family business at both places before opening up his own place in Fayetteville on July 7, 1957.

Back then, Fayetteville had 8,000 residents and one traffic light. Today, there are more than 100,000 people in Fayette County. Needless to say, there have been a lot of changes, and Ken has seen them all. Odds are pretty good he catered at them, too.

Kenneth's is where it's always been, on the corner of State Highway 85 and what is now Melear's Way. The oak and hickory is stacked long and high, making a fence around the barbecue pit, which is housed in a covered shed.

Across the parking lot is Melear's Barbecue. The cinderblocks are painted in an alternate black and white checker pattern, reminiscent of the flag that signifies that the race has been won.

"I'm a big NASCAR fan," Kenneth proudly proclaims. The interior walls are practically a

NASCAR museum. It must be pointed out that there is trouble in paradise. Kenneth is a huge Jeff Gordon fan, and his wife, Merrium, pulls for Dale Jr.

That aside, a lot of the fun of Melear's is eating off those turquoise school-cafeteria trays, circa 1960.

"The elementary school called me up and told me they were going to be getting rid of them and if I'd be interested. I bought all 700 of them for a dime apiece. You can't break them, and they divide the food up perfectly."

NOT EXACTLY THEIR BRUNSWICK STEW

2 pounds beef, roast or chuck

2 pounds Boston butt

2 pounds chicken

3 (15-ounce) cans whole corn

3 (15-ounce) cans creamed corn

2 (15-ounce) cans lima beans

2 (14-ounce) cans diced new potatoes

46 ounces ketchup

2 (28-ounce) cans whole tomatoes

2 large yellow onions, finely chopped

8 ounces Worcestershire sauce

5 ounces Texas Pete hot sauce

2 (18-ounce) bottles tomato-based
   barbecue sauce

Fully cook the meat (smoking is preferred). Combine all the other ingredients in a stockpot, 16-quart or larger. Bring to a boil and then turn to low heat for about 2 hours. Be sure to stir periodically so that it doesn't burn on the bottom of the pot. Finely chop up the cooked meat—a Cuisinart is especially good for this. Stir chopped meat into the pot for the final 10 minutes of cooking and mix thoroughly. Serves 20–25, but you can halve the recipe. Freezes especially well.

"MY BARBECUE IS SO GOOD, IT'LL MAKE A FREIGHT TRAIN STOP RIGHT IN ITS TRACKS."

That's not hyperbole, but fact. It is not uncommon for the train that runs behind this joint to stop for a quick to-go order.

"I started out by selling boiled peanuts and tomatoes right here on this corner," Don Bryant, aka "Mountain Man," told me. "Then I started selling barbecue. Then I got this '73 Bluebird School bus that was partially converted into a kitchen. I drove it here and here it's been ever since. The shelter and tables have kind of grown up around it."

Don has seen a lot of changes to Flowery Branch over his fourteen years. His used to be the only place to get a quick bite to eat if you don't count the filling station. His landlord was so appreciative to have him around, he gave him a very low lifetime lease for as long as he stays. "He even lent me the money to get the bus. I paid him back in six months."

Don's joint is on the corner of Atlanta Highway and a stretch of Sprout Springs Road that is known as Phil Niekro Boulevard. (That's Hall of Famer Phil Niekro, who along with fellow knuckle-baller Joe, won more games than any other brother combination in Major League Baseball history.) And if you're lucky, you'll see the famed pitcher. He stops by just about every day.

Recently, there have been storm clouds on the horizon. The sleepy little town of Flowery Branch is one hour north of Atlanta, the poster child of urban sprawl. It is only a matter of time before that tidal wave washes over, leaving in its wake their sensibilities wrapped in McMansions and tract housing.

Case in point: the health inspector forced Don to put a roof over his smoker, enclose it in a screen and place it on a concrete slab. Progress?

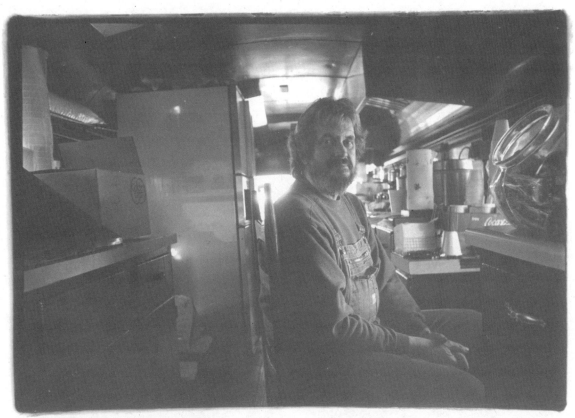

"MOUNTAIN MAN" DON BRYANT'S BOILED PEANUTS

10 pounds raw dried peanuts

4 cups iodized salt

8 gallons water (to start)

It is important that you use a stainless steel pot because of the amount of salt required.

You will want to cook the peanuts outside over a wood or propane fire. As wonderful as the smell is, it is overwhelming indoors. Note where water level is when starting. You will be adding water periodically.

Day 1. Boil peanuts in water for a good 12 hours, or until soft. Add water as needed.

Day 2. Add salt, and bring water up to 8 gallon level. Boil for about 12 hours. Add water as needed.

"HAVEN'T HAD ONE FIGHT SINCE WE BECAME A BARBECUE JOINT,"

Steve Connor told me after recommending the blackberry cobbler.

I remember this place when it was a back-woods juke joint called "The Sundance." I was a counselor at a nearby summer camp and was warned not to go there, but if we did, we best not talk to any of the women there. "You just might get a pool cue upside your head, or worse." Needless to say, we went.

It was everything a juke joint should be. Pool, beer, local talent on open mic with a loud, good-timey crowd.

Twenty years later the beer, pool tables and cigarettes are gone. The only thing smoking in this joint are the hams and ribs. In its place is a clean, well-lit, family-style establishment. Sue Connor just got tired of the hassle.

"Been there, done that," she says.

Steve used to work for the Department of Transportation, where he was an animal trapper for the twenty-one counties of Northeast Georgia. He may be retired from the state, but he still is the man to call if you have bear problems.

"I'm well known around here and get calls at

all hours. It is against the law to kill a bear in Georgia [unlike North Carolina, which is fifteen miles up 441]. So me and my dogs just run them off."

Calling this a "family-style" joint would be an understatement. Son Neil, manages the back. He is the 'cue master. Before he was shooing flies at the pits, he was shoeing horses and laying bricks. His wife Beth manages the front. There are also grandkids who have the run of the place.

Sue tells me, "This is much better. It seems like all the stories at the Sundance involved guns and knives. Now it's all good. My favorite story from this place happened one evening. It was crowded and I was helping seat people. We have a couple of long benches, and when it gets crowded, I just have to put people where I can find space. I put this one guy at an open seat and he looked at the guy across from him, and he noticed that he looked familiar. The other guy had the same reaction. It turns out they were old Vietnam War buddies and had actually tried to contact each other over the years, but couldn't find each other until they came here."

The sun may have set on the Sundance, but its soul lives on in Oinkers.

STEVE CONNOR OF OINKER'S BARBECUED BEAR (YES, BEAR)

3-pound bear roast, either ham or shoulder cut

1 quart water

1 quart barbecue sauce

Cook bear meat in a slow cooker with water for 6 hours on high heat. Drain water and then cut roast into chunks. Put back slow cooker with barbecue sauce and cook for 2 more hours on low heat.

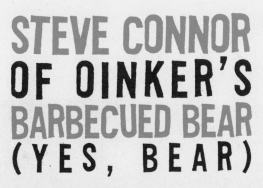

"THIS PLACE SHOULD HAVE BEEN CALLED THE SHIMMY SHACK,"

Bonnie Combs tells me. "Because every time a train goes by, the whole place shakes."

Being located next to the railroad line, on the outskirts of the Okefenokee Swamp, Bonnie explains that, "It's only by the grace of God and word of mouth that people find their way here. We are so far off the interstate."

This little shack buried deep in the woods looks like something straight out of a 1930s cartoon, with its bright lights and anthropomorphic ice cream cones made out of plywood. The kids might be screaming, "When will we get there?!", but they will beg you to bring them back here. That said, don't be fooled. They dish up some serious backwoods 'cue.

This funhouse with a soul started out as strictly an ice-cream place. The Combs acquired it when Bonnie got laid off at Anchor Glass in Jacksonville.

Dwight didn't think much about it except as something to keep Bonnie busy, but in a later reorganization of the company he worked for, he was demoted from forklift operator to box stacker.

"That was something I did the day I walked in to that place twenty-four years ago. I was a year away from retirement and a gold watch, but I couldn't take going into that place anymore and I already had a watch, so I just quit. I really didn't think it through, because business just died in the winter. Nobody wants ice cream that time of year. That's when we added the barbecue," Dwight tells me.

Not only did he add the barbecue, but he built on to the shack, using salvaged wood from other abandoned barns and sheds. "It's all fatlighter wood," Dwight points out. "It lasts forever as long as the termites don't get to it. I have to spray it once a year."

Dwight is a very soft spoken and modest man. Not one to toot his own horn. He might call it a shack, but the craftsmanship is excellent. He built his smoker with help from his late brother Jimmy. It

was so sturdy that Bonnie and her mother could not open the door without a struggle. They complained about it and he attached a garage door opener to the smoker's door. "Now all I have to do is push a button. People have heard about it and stopped by just to see it," Bonnie proudly states.

"And to pick up some good barbecue and ice cream," Dwight adds with a sly smile.

SHACK BY THE TRACK'S BUTTERSCOTCH SQUARES

1 cup butter

1 pound brown sugar

1 teaspoon vanilla extract

2 large eggs

2 cups self-rising flour

1 cup chopped nuts, walnuts or pecans (optional)

Preheat oven to 350 degrees.

Melt butter; add sugar and mix well. Stir in vanilla, eggs, flour, and optional nuts. Bake in a 9 x 13-inch pan for 30 minutes. Cool, then cut into squares.

Williams' Barbeque
15 Highway 98 East • Danielsville, GA 30633 • (706) 795-5394

"THE BOSS SAID THAT HE'D BE BACK IN TWO WEEKS,"

Ricky Williams tells me as he scoops the perfect amount of chili on a hot dog.

"That was seventeen years ago. I'd been driving propane trucks. On my route, I saw this old man with a barbecue trailer. It had a 'For Sale' sign on it. I found out his health was not good, and that he was looking to get out. I bought the trailer and took over his corner."

Ricky always appreciated good barbecue. He used to get together with his buddies and smoke a whole hog over a few cold ones.

Ricky keeps it simple. "There's no fryer. You can get a glass of tea, but Cokes are in the machine by the ordering window." For dessert, they proudly serve Moon Pies.

"A few years back, I built this kitchen with a take-out window." As humble as it is today, "It was like going from a telephone booth into a mansion," Ricky says as he taps the plywood ceiling. The ambiance is complete with satellite radio piping in the R & B.

Helping Ricky for the past decade is Cooter

Baxter. She had been a seamstress, but then they shipped her job overseas. Not wanting to leave the area, she took a job at Hardee's across the street.

"I hated it. They treated me like a kid. I lasted only three months.

"I love everything about this job. This is the best job I ever had. I'll never leave here," Cooter says with conviction.

"If and when she ever leaves, I'll be right behind her," Ricky adds.

RICKY WILLIAMS' HOT DOG CHILI

1-1/2 pounds ground beef

1 teaspoon salt

1 (29-ounce) can tomato sauce

2 teaspoons vinegar

2 tablespoons chili powder

2-1/2 teaspoons Worcestershire

2 teaspoons cumin

1 teaspoon garlic powder

Do not brown meat first! Combine all ingredients together. Cook on high heat until boiling, mixing to break up meat. Cover and stir occasionally on low heat for about 45 minutes. Spoon over hot dogs in buns.

"THIS IS OVER. I WANT YOU TO PLAY FOR ME."

That is what Richard Street heard through the crowd noise as he stepped to the plate with the bases loaded that sunny Sunday afternoon in the summer of 1980. Richard was a semi-pro baseball player.

"I couldn't hit. Tears of joy came to my eyes. My baseball career was over. Jesus had a plan for me."

That next Sunday, Richard was at trial sermon. The next month he was enrolled in the seminary.

"I have been anointed to do, and to reach out to people . . . to be an example."

After graduation, Richard was assigned to a small congregation in Union Springs, Alabama. He led them for fourteen years, preaching, among other things, self-reliance, which he put into practice with a church farm and businesses. This led to a falling out with his bishop, because he refused to receive a salary. "I do not take money for God's work."

Richard started his own church, "The Streets of Gold Interdenominational Church," in Midway, Alabama. They began in a double-wide, but hard work and blessings raised $38,000 to literally build their church, which was completed in 2001.

Pastor Richard was led by God to acquire a strip mall a few miles down the road in the Wynnton area of Columbus, Georgia. Today, that houses the church's businesses. In addition to the barbecue restaurant, there is a hauling/road building outfit, a braid shop, and a barber shop. The latter is where you are most likely to find Richard during the day, dispensing God's word and haircuts.

"All this is through Christ; he tells me to do, and I do. He gave me the recipe for my coleslaw and sauce (a mustard/vinegar base). People come from all over to buy it by the gallon. The soldiers in Fort Benning come in here and, when they get deployed, they want us to ship it to them. We send it all over the world. We are in the process of patenting and putting it on the market."

73

MISS DORIS DAVIS'S
OF WYNNTON PITT BBQ & RESTAURANT'S
OLD—FASHIONED
CORNBREAD STUFFING

4-1/2 cups cornbread crumbs

2-1/2 cups white bread crumbs

1 cup chopped onion

1 cup chopped celery

1/4 cup butter (melted)

2 to 3 cups hot chicken broth

1/2 teaspoon black pepper

4 eggs

1/2 cup buttermilk

1 teaspoon sugar

Pour breadcrumbs into a large pan. In a frying pan, lightly saute onion and celery in butter. Add to crumb mixture. Add other ingredients and mix well. If dressing seems too dry, add more broth. Bake in a shallow pan at 400 degrees for 15 to 20 minutes. Mix well and enjoy.

"I CAN SEE YOU'RE PRETTY, I'LL JUST HAVE TO FIND OUT ABOUT HONEST AND DEPENDABLE."

That is how Carol Avery was described by a friend to Walter Ford—as pretty, honest and dependable. He had just bought George's Bar-B-Q and needed to hire a waitress.

Carol was doing office work at the time and had

been a waitress in the past. She mentioned that she would like to get back into waitressing part time. Her friend told her to go see Walter.

"You'll really like him. He's a great guy," the friend said.

Walter hired her on the spot. They hit it off right from the start. They both realized that their

friendship transcended George's. A year and a half later, they were Mr. and Mrs. Ford.

Today, Carol spends most of her time running George's and Walter splits his time there and tending cattle on their 200 acres.

Walter bought George's in 1989. It was a venerable Owensboro establishment started in 1955, but it had recently changed hands a couple of times.

"I had a video and frame shop across the street and would eat there often. The owner approached me about taking it over. He just wanted to get out. I had never thought about it, but the cook, Orville Horn, agreed to stay on and show me the business if I bought it, so I did.

"Orville was a great cook and he became a really good friend until he died a few years back, but he lacked a little in the customer relations department. I'll never forget soon after I just

bought the place. Back then they would take raw meat from people to smoke. The only stipulation was that the meat be thawed out and ready to throw on the smoker—we couldn't have it sitting around thawing. This woman brought in some meat that was frozen solid and Orville told her to go home, thaw it out, and come back.

"She responded, 'If I leave here with this meat I ain't coming back.'

To which Orville replied, 'I don't care if you come back or not.'

"I couldn't believe what I just saw, and I tried, unsuccessfully, to apologize and explain the situation, but she would have none of it. I'm thinking, what have I got myself into. I'm not going to be in business if my employees treat people like that, so I tried to explain that to Orville and he just said, 'Bitch should have known better' and walked away."

WESTERN KENTUCKY BURGOO

Mutton is virtually impossible to find outside of Western Kentucky, where it is a favorite dish. It is the key ingredient in burgoo, which is widely enjoyed in that neck of the woods. This recipe was published in the *Louisville Courier-Journal*. It was taken from the cookbook *Owensboro's Very Famous Moonlite Bar-B-Q Inn Inc.*

4 pounds mutton

1 (3-pound) chicken

3/4 pound cabbage, ground or chopped fine

3/4 pound onion, ground or chopped fine

5 pounds potatoes, peeled and diced

2 (17-ounce) cans corn or 2 cups fresh corn

3/4 cup ketchup

3 (10.75-ounce) cans tomato puree

juice of 1 lemon

3/4 cup distilled vinegar

1/2 cup Worcestershire sauce

2-1/2 tablespoons salt, or to taste

2 tablespoons black pepper

1 teaspoon cayenne pepper (more if you like)

(Some area cooks add dried beans or lima beans, tomatoes, and a little boiled, shredded beef or wild game.)

Boil mutton in enough water to cover. Cook until tender, 2 to 3 hours. Discard broth and bones. Chop meat fine; set aside. Boil chicken. Add cabbage, onion, potatoes, corn, ketchup and 1 gallon water to chicken broth. (If you are following the area cooks' recipe, add those ingredients now.) Bring to a boil.

Meanwhile, chop chicken meat and discard bones and skin. When potatoes are tender, add chopped chicken, mutton, tomato puree, lemon juice, vinegar, Worcestershire sauce, salt, black pepper, and cayenne pepper. Simmer for 2 hours or longer, stirring occasionally as it thickens.

JACK EASLEY MAY HAVE LEFT TEACHING, BUT HE NEVER QUIT BEING A TEACHER.

He is a soft spoken, mountain of a man that you wouldn't want to cross or disappoint. "I taught physical education and coached football and baseball at the Breckinridge Job Corp Center—it was a vocational school. The juvenile courts would send kids there from all over the country, but mostly they were from the Northeast—New York, New Jersey, Philadelphia.

"They were not bad kids. They came from bad places with no structure or positive role models. We took them out of that environment and gave them structure and taught them a useful trade. Things like auto mechanics, welding, carpentry and landscaping. It was rewarding work."

Marion, Kentucky is not just a different environment, it is another world: clean air, small-town Amish country in the western part of the state not far from the banks of the Ohio River.

"My wife and I are from here. It is the kind of place where people look out for each other. If you get into any sort of trouble, people will help you out."

This from a man who always answered the bell as a volunteer fireman for twenty years.

"I don't get around as well as I used to. I had both knees replaced in '02 and my left has been replaced twice. These are residual effects from high school football injuries. They don't keep me from playing golf every Wednesday with my group."

Jack coached football at the local high school where they were Class A State Champs in 1985. "When my son entered, I quit. I don't think it's right to coach your own."

Jack runs a small, efficient operation. Most of his business is take-out, but Jack built a screened-in covered dining area if you want to make it a picnic. He's helped by his wife Judy and their son, Mark. She recently retired from teaching first and second grades in Marion for thirty-three years.

Being on the edge of the barbecue belt, they get a lot of questions, like "What is barbecue?" Jack felt he didn't have the time to adequately answer the question, so he wrote a small booklet explaining it, along with recipes and instructions on how to build your own pit. Like I said, he never quit teaching.

JACK (THAT USED TO BE BY THE TRACKS) EASLEY'S TOMATO-BASED BARBECUE SAUCE

2 cups ketchup

1 cup distilled white vinegar

1 cup sugar

1/2 cup yellow mustard

1/2 stick butter

2 tablespoons concentrated lemon juice

2 tablespoons chili powder

2 tablespoons salt

1 tablespoon black pepper

1 tablespoon red pepper

1 tablespoon A-1 steak sauce

Mix all ingredients together and heat to a boil in a 2-quart saucepan. Remove from heat and cool. Stored in the refrigerator, can last several months. Makes about a quart.

"IT'S NOW OR NEVER,"

Ken Ramage told me over a big glass of tea.

"I grew up in Paducah where my dad was a bricklayer by trade, but always loved to barbecue. He combined the two by opening up his Plantation Barbecue. I had a lot of fond memories of that place as a kid. It burned down in 1953. I have a mass of nickels all melted together from that fire."

Murvin Ramage never did reopen—he went back to laying brick—but he was highly sought after to build pits, which he did all over Western Kentucky.

Ken's dream of opening up a barbecue restaurant was put on hold. He got drafted and served in Vietnam, where he earned a Purple Heart. As part of his recovery, he was sent to Louisville, where he met Sharon, who was a singer in the U.S.O. They married, settled down, and Ken took a job on the railroad.

"I had just turned forty and I knew if I waited any longer I wouldn't have the energy to do it, so I enlisted the help from my dad and we built this place from the ground up. I couldn't have done it without him."

They built in an open industrial part of town. It has plenty of room for the trees that lie in Purgatory at the edge of their parking lot, waiting to be carved up and burned in the pits.

Like their building, everything at the Ole Hickory

Pit is made from scratch. Sharon specializes in the baked goods, which are made fresh daily.

Son Mike gets into the act in his own unique way. He is very proud of his hot sauces. He literally makes them from the ground up, growing his own peppers. "I got red, black, habaneros, jalapeños, Scotch bonnets, cayenne, vasicio and even one called Macho Camacho," he says.

They have not had any fires, but the local fire department gets together there for their monthly meetings. Sharon told me with a big smile, "One of those times, a local television news reporter was driving by and saw our lot filled with fire trucks. He thought that he was first on the scene. Was he disappointed when he found out that there was no fire!"

"HIGHWAY 90 IS NOT THE DANKEN TRAIL."

"This place was called The Hitching Post when my partner Ken and I bought it. We just put our names together and stuck with the western theme."

You might be a bit disappointed if you want to whet your whistle on a good sarsaparilla, but you won't be disappointed if you've got a hankering for some fine barbecue.

Dan Bannister came from Monroe. After eighteen years as a commercial deep-sea diver, often going to depths of 500 feet and being away from home for three months at a time, he was ready to start a new phase of his life on dry land.

"Owning a barbecue joint is not as dangerous as diving, but it is every bit as crazy. My partner bailed on me and I was fortunate to have Patricia and our five kids to help out."

Dan met Patricia in Hawaii, where he was stationed in the Navy and she was a student.

"I just went up to her and asked for a date. I must have looked good in a uniform, because she said yes.

"It turned out that she was from Haynesville. I knew her cousin and we had mutual friends. I went off to Vietnam for two years and didn't keep up

with her, but when I came back home to Monroe, I looked her up. She was still around. Five months later, we were married.

"I have a no-compromise policy here. I don't compromise on my food or the service. We do everything the right way. It takes a lot of hard work, but it pays off in the long run, with loyal customers and little employee turnover."

Managing the place for the past dozen years is Delores Crowe, or as everyone calls her, "Miss D." She is assisted by Dewayne Simmons, or "Double D." He has been with Dan since he was fourteen, when he would come by to cut the grass. Eighteen years later, he does just about everything else at The Danken Trail.

This location of The Danken Trail will be coming to an end soon. Dan will be breaking ground on a new building next door.

"This place was run down the day I bought it twenty-five years ago, but we got as much as we could out of it."

Maybe the new building should be called "D's Place." Just a suggestion.

CAJUN RED BEANS AND RICE
(NOT ON THEIR MENU)

1 stalk celery

1 green bell pepper

1 large yellow onion

1 pound good-quality rope sausage

4 bay leaves

2 tablespoons chili powder

2 tablespoons cumin

4 tablespoons paprika

2 pounds dry light-red or pinto beans (do not soak overnight)

Chop celery, bell pepper and onion to small dice. Cut sausage into small quarter-size pieces. Saute until onion turns translucent.

Put into large 2-gallon-plus pot. Add bay leaves, chili powder, cumin and paprika. Wash beans and add to pot. Stir well to keep veggies and sausage from burning.

Add about 1-1/2 gallons of water. Bring to a boil. Reduce heat to medium and cover. Cook until the beans are soft (about 2 hours). Add salt, pepper and hot sauce to taste here—because their content varies greatly in the sausage. Serve over cooked rice.

Avoid soaking the beans overnight because that will start a fermentation process that is very undesirable.

"GRANDMA HAD THE DEACON'S FAMILY OVER FOR DINNER EVERY SUNDAY,"

says Virginia Johnson.

"As a girl growing up in Centerville, Mississippi, I would help my mother and grandmother out in the kitchen. I would watch them cook. They didn't use recipes. They would reach for this and that. They didn't measure ingredients, but knew exactly the right amount to put in. They would let me help out and give me specific instructions, like exactly how many times to beat the batter. When I started baking on my own, I tried to copy them, with mixed results. They could always tell exactly what was wrong. 'Too much lemon shavings, not enough sugar, a pinch more baking powder . . .' It was very frustrating, because they never wrote anything down, but now, I'm the same way. You can call it a gift, but I worked very hard to acquire it."

It was an irrefutable fact that the Hyster women could cook, and after much encouragement, they opened up a restaurant 150 miles down the road in New Orleans, a city renowned for its food. Hyster's Bar-B-Que opened its doors in 1972.

"They went there to make money, but they never left Centerville. That was always home, and they would return every weekend."

At that time, Virginia had started studying political science—first at Southern University, then Atlanta University for a master's degree.

Always fond of school, she embarked on a fifteen-year teaching career and was contemplating law school, but jurisprudence's loss was culinary's gain, for the pull of the family and her gift for cooking proved too great.

Nothing could stop her from her calling—not even Hurricane Katrina, which came through, broke the levees, and washed her beloved business and town away.

"There was no question about re-opening. I came back and worked twelve to fifteen hours

a day for two months. During that time I refused to listen to the news. It was just too depressing. To get through we only played spiritual music."

At the time of publication, the surrounding neighborhood still had a long way to go, but it is slowly coming back. Hyster's is literally a beacon of hope. It is an actual living, breathing museum of antiques and African-American artifacts. A place where the neighborhood can go to be reminded of what it was like and, with love and hard work, can become again.

VIRGINIA JOHNSON'S GREENS WASHING TIP

Washing greens is serious business at Ms. Hyster's Barbecue in New Orleans. Virginia washes at least six dozen bunches a day and is vigilant about her process.

Greens are funnel shaped, and as they emerge from the ground, they scoop up a lot of soil. Also, insects find their dense, leafy foliage to be a safe haven.

First Virginia "picks 'em" by removing the stems. Then she fills three large basins with cold water. She puts a tablespoon of salt in the first one (she says that the salt brings the bugs to the top), all the while working the greens with her hands.

She then moves them to the second sink, where the remaining grit and excess green pigment gets washed out. By the time she moves them to the third sink, the water should be crystal clear.

Most kitchens have dual sinks, so after that first washing with salt, empty and replace the water with fresh cold water. By the time the greens hit the second sink (third dunking), the water should have that crystal clarity so important for proper greens preparation.

Uncle Buck's Smoke House
2920 Jewella Avenue • Shreveport, LA 71109 • (318) 635-5184

"YOU MUST BE LOOKING FOR THE RESTAURANT. JUST GO THROUGH THAT DOOR."

I had been told about Buck's legendary ribs, but when I walk in, I see a dimly lit bar, a dance floor with disco ball spinning, a foxy lady on the wall. I saw the sign for Uncle Buck's Restaurant, but this was not what I was expecting. The waitress saw that perplexed look before, and she set me straight.

I passed from a world where you had to be twenty-one to enter, into a restaurant that serves family-style meals.

"I always wanted to own a club and a barbecue joint," Ben "Buck" Banks tells me.

"I was a trucker during the week, but on the weekend, I was always smoking ribs. A friend of mine had this barbecue joint and he wanted out so bad that he offered it to me for $150. That was back in 1978."

Carolyn added, "I had always worked in restaurants around town, so I was very skeptical at first. I knew how much work a restaurant is, but I would come in and help out. I started spending more and more time here, and expanding the menu. I really enjoyed having a place of our own, and after about six months, he just turned this place over to me."

With Carolyn and the family holding down the restaurant, Ben set his sights on that club that he always wanted.

"I would drive a truck all during the week. After work on Friday, I'd go straight to the restaurant and smoke ribs all night. I'd spend Saturday splitting time between the club and the restaurant, and spend my Sundays at the club."

Over the years, the club and the restaurant moved locations a couple of times, which kept Ben hopping, but today, they are under one roof, which is a lot easier on Ben. Now that he isn't trucking anymore, he has more time to pursue his fishing hobby.

When Carolyn is not at the restaurant cooking, you can find her at church. She plays serious bingo at least two nights a week.

"ABE'S IS INDEED LOCATED ON HALLOWED GROUND."

61 49 Situated right at the historic crossroads, Abe's is keeping the spirit alive.

As legend has it, Robert Johnson picked up a barbecue sandwich from the back door of the Delta Inn, sat under a sycamore tree and, at those very crossroads, made a deal with the devil. In exchange for his eternal soul, the devil gave Robert (and mankind) the blues.

"A lot of things have changed since the Jim Crow South. Blacks and whites are no longer forbidden by law to dine in the same establishment. The Delta Inn was renamed Abe's, in honor of my father, but you can still get the same great sandwich with our distinctive sauce," Pat Davis Sr. told me. "It is truly the stuff of legend."

That is not the only legend that shrouds Abe's. In 1913, Pat Sr.'s Lebanese grandfather, Habeeb, sent his thirteen-year-old son, Abe, his eleven-year-old son, Joe, and his nine-year-old daughter, Mary, to America to join their mother, Sadie, to peddle clothes. He remained in Lebanon because he had a vision that he would be struck and killed by a large block of iron if he made the journey to America.

Abe did not take to selling clothes, but he did eventually end up in Clarksdale, where he went to work for a Greek restaurateur. He found working in a restaurant much more to his liking and eventually opened up his own place, the Bungalow Inn, in 1924.

The Bungalow Inn was not an inn but a restaurant, and a very successful one at that. In 1937, it was relocated to its current location at the famed crossroads. Abe also renamed it the Delta Inn. It was renamed Abe's in 1960 by Pat Sr., to honor the memory of his father.

As far as the other legend goes, Abe and his mother convinced Habeeb that America was a wonderful place and that he should come here. Habeeb put his fear aside and journeyed to America. When he arrived in Clarksdale, he stepped off on the wrong side of the train and was promptly run over by another train.

When you visit The Crossroads and Abe's in Clarksdale, be sure to stop by the Delta Blues Museum. There you can find out more about Robert Johnson and his disciples Howlin' Wolf, Muddy Waters and B. B. King. They went on to inspire other artists such as The Rolling Stones, Eric Clapton and the ZZ Top dudes.

ABE'S COLESLAW

Coleslaw that doesn't drown out the flavor of meat, but enhances the taste.

1 cabbage, cored and shredded (or use 2 pounds pre-shredded cabbage)

2 teaspoons salt

1 teaspoon black pepper

6 ounces white vinegar

3 ounces vegetable oil

Mix all ingredients together; refrigerate at least 2 hours. Season more if desired.

"IF YOU CAN MANAGE A $4 MILLION BUDGET, YOU CAN SURE MANAGE THIS."

That's what Demetris Buck told S.B. when he was thinking about buying his friend's restaurant.

"I was just laid off, 'downsized' by Cooper Tools, where I was a manager. That was back in '96."

S.B. has always enjoyed cooking. He's been doing it all his life. He grew up on the Billups Plantation outside of Indianola, Mississippi (where B.B. King is from). It was there he learned to cook from his mother. "She taught me how to use seasonings, not salt and pepper. There were thirteen of us, so I know how to cook for lots of people.

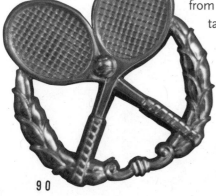

"Even though I knew I could cook, and even the managing of people, it was tough-going at first. The location was terrible. We had to move. It was just soul food back then. I added the barbecue. Now, we serve breakfast, a cafeteria style lunch, and short orders after 2:30. We also do fish fries and catering, and I'm still trying to figure this out."

You don't expect to see tennis trophies and memorabilia at a soul food/barbecue joint, especially in the middle of the Mississippi Delta, but S.B. fell in love with the game. "I was twenty-five years old and was fishing with my brother when we decided we would like to learn how to play."

S.B. is now a USPTR teaching pro. He is very proud that he has helped thirteen kids go to college on tennis scholarships, including both of his kids.

Like so many other things in life, the risk of opening up a family restaurant can pay off with big dividends down the road. A few years after S.B. lost his job, the same thing happened to Demetris. After she had put in nineteen years on the assembly line at Utility Product, they abruptly closed the plant.

"I was always helping out here anyway. Now this became my full-time job," she says.

Demetris is also quite a cook in her own right. A lifelong Greenville resident, she also learned the art from her mother.

Her love for this place is evident in the way she cuts up with everybody.

"I always get a kick out of hearing how people are surprised when they find out I'm the owner, as if that means you can't have fun just because you're the boss.

"But my absolute favorite time here is when we are visited by the grandkids. They live in Jackson, and when they come over, they help clean tables and stuff their faces."

S.B. BUCK'S MACARONI & CHEESE

3 cups uncooked macaroni

4 eggs

2 cups whole milk

1/2 cup flour

1/2 cup sugar

1 teaspoon salt

1 teaspoon pepper

1-1/2 cups grated sharp cheddar, divided

Preheat oven to 350 degrees.

Boil macaroni according to package directions; wash to get starch off.

Mix all ingredients together except 1/2 cup cheese, adding macaroni last. Combine in an oven-safe pan and sprinkle remaining cheese on top. Cook for 20 minutes. Serves 8 to 10 people.

"A LIGHT BULB WENT OFF."

"I was eating at this little Italian restaurant after my shift. It was one of those small, family-owned places where they served the food that they grew up on. Not fancy, but real."

Bob Hamil was not one to react to fleeting impulses. He had worked very hard to become a police officer, getting a degree in criminal justice from Southern Mississippi University in Hattiesburg. So when he told his wife, Jeanne, whom he had known since high school, she understood and was very supportive.

Nor was he completely naive. His father, Gene, had a similar experience, first buying into Ossie's, a regional hamburger/barbecue chain, in the mid-60s, then opening up the original Hamil's.

"I'll never forget the day we first opened up—August 23, 1977. Somebody came into the place and announced that Elvis had just died," Edith Hamil remembers.

The cabin that Gene built for Edith has served the Hamils well over the years—first as a furniture store, and now as the restaurant. When Bob came back thirteen years ago, he really invigorated the sleepy little family place on the outskirts of town. It is now so insufficient that folks can't get in and out during their allotted lunch hour. This oft-heard complaint will soon be a thing of the past, once they open up the new Mamma Hamil's directly behind the soon-to-be-retired cabin/restaurant.

"I don't want our new place to be all new. I still want it to have the connection to the town and the people. We've been planning this for a

while, and have been stockpiling materials salvaged from a lot of the old buildings that have been torn down around here. We will have exposed walls that are made from the bleachers of the old Madison High School football stadium," Bob proudly states.

Edith adds, "I can feel Jesus's love flow through this place like a river."

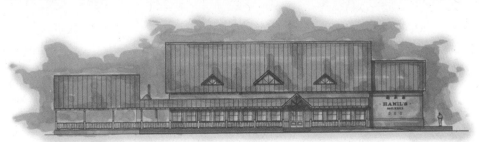

MAMMA HAMIL'S WATERMELON RIND PICKLES

Rind from 1 big melon

7 cups sugar

2 cups apple cider vinegar

1/2 teaspoon cinnamon oil

1/2 teaspoon clove oil

First Day: After you eat the watermelon, trim the rind from the red meat and green outside. Cut into 1-inch cubes. Parboil for 10 minutes in enough water to cover. Drain off water and put rind in large bowl.

In another bowl, mix all other ingredients together. Bring mixture to a boil and then pour over rind; cover and let stand overnight.

Second Day: Drain juice off rind. Heat that juice to a boil and then pour over rind and let stand overnight again.

Third Day: Drain juice off rind again and heat to a boil. Put in jars with rind and seal. Refrigerate and enjoy in 3 more days.

"I'VE ALWAYS LOVED THE BLUES AND BARBECUE,"

Lindsay Shannon tells me on the front porch of his joint.

"I remember as a kid in the early '60s going to the Kansas City A's games at the old Municipal

Stadium. I'd go grab a barbecue sandwich and a bleacher seat. The whole thing cost about four bucks."

A lot has changed since then. The A's left town. Municipal Stadium is long gone, but you can still get some really great 'cue in KC. It just costs a little more.

Lindsay started barbecuing in high school and continued at college. "It was hard to find good barbecue in Philadelphia, but I did find a great joint, Bea Bea's Lawnside. It was in a tough neighborhood. I always got a kick that it was called

'Lawnside' since there was no grass or trees."

Lindsay did eventually return to Kansas City, where he sold ad space on billboards. He also met and married Jo, who did public relations.

Ever the blues freak, Lindsay was frustrated when he couldn't find it on KC radio. He approached the local public radio station about hosting his own show in '77. That lasted nine years; then he brought the show over to commercial radio, where it still is today. Along the way he helped establish the first Kansas City Blues Festival in 1980. "I was also barbecuing for the festival on fifty-five gallon drum barrels," he adds with a laugh.

It took Lindsay nearly ten years, but he finally made the leap and opened up his own place in 1990. "It was only a matter of time," Jo says.

She soon said farewell to the corporate world to join him. She handles the accounting and ordering. "The back of the house," as Lindsay puts it. "I take care of the front."

He named his place after the original Bea Bea's, keeping the authenticity by locating it in a fifty-year-old building. True to the original Lawnside, there is no lawn or trees. He did change Bea Bea's to just the initials B.B.'s, but Lindsay would not confirm or deny my suspicion that he did this after the blues legend B.B. King.

The Shannons got it right, mixing live blues and barbecue and sprinkling a little Cajun in for good measure. They really succeeded in bringing a diverse group of folks together. It is not uncommon to see hardcore bikers next to suburban families next to blues lovers—all having a wonderful time.

LINDSAY SHANNON'S
B.B.'S LAWNSIDE
BARBECUE GUMBO

You can use any kind of smoked meat such as pork, beef, chicken, iguana . . . served over rice.

2 large yellow onions	Salt and ground black pepper to taste
2 green bell peppers	1 cup water
1/2 bunch celery	2 (28-ounce) cans crushed tomatoes
1 cup okra	3 cups chicken stock
4 pounds barbecued meat scraps	2 teaspoons red pepper
6 tablespoons butter	3 tablespoons Worcestershire sauce
1/2 teaspoon garlic powder	1 tablespoon Louisiana-style hot sauce

Peel and chop onions and then core, seed and chop peppers. Trim and chop celery and then cut okra; chop barbecue meat.

Melt butter in a large pot over medium-low heat. Add onions, bell peppers, celery and okra; cook, stirring occasionally, until soft (about 20 minutes). Add garlic powder and season with salt and pepper. Increase heat to high, then add water, meat, tomatoes, and chicken stock to pot. Bring to a boil, then reduce heat to medium-low and simmer until meat is fork-tender and falling apart (about 30 minutes). Add okra, red pepper, Worcestershire sauce and Louisiana hot sauce (more if you like) and continue cooking until okra is tender and gumbo has thickened. Serve over rice.

"I'M THROWED IN THE RIVER, I GOTTA SWIM."

Farmland Industrial, a processor of pork products, was in the midst of a severe downturn. L.C. Richardson was a chef at their corporate headquarters.

"It was a job that I really enjoyed, but they put together a really nice package, so I took early retirement. It gave me the opportunity to do this, which was something I was thinking about doing for a long time. Now I had no excuse."

He bought a building that used to be a liquor store, and L.C.'s Bar-B-Q was born.

"I started cooking outside with a little cooker. It was just me, and let me tell you, it could get really hot in the summer and cold in the winter out there.

"The insurance and the health inspectors did not like that set-up, so I had to bring the smoker indoors."

Running a barbecue joint makes for some very long days. L.C. had to give up the other job he enjoyed, working as a buffet chef at the Royals' Stadium Club. "They haven't been the same since," L.C. says with a big old laugh.

That is an undeniable truth. The Royals had just won the 1985 World Series. Since then, they have become perennial cellar dwellers.

Farmland Industries' and the Royals' loss has been Kansas City's gain. In a town already known for excellent barbecue, there is always room for another great place. It is a point that has not gone unnoticed by the Kansas City Star, which has consistently given L.C.'s joint four stars, its highest rating.

L.C. did not give up his other love. The place is filled with his hunting and fishing trophies. He goes out every chance he gets. Success in barbecue has enabled him to pursue his passion even further. In fact, when I met him he had just got back from a fishing trip in Canada.

"I want to write a book, *From the Call to the Kitchen*. It would be all about duck hunting—from outfitting and tracking to preparing and cooking."

L.C. is a big teddy bear of a man. Like the smoke that permeates the joint, he has truly surrounded himself with things that he loves. He has at least ten family members helping him out. That frees him up to go on the trips that he cherishes so much.

L.C. RICHARDSON'S SWEET & SOUR WILD GAME AND DOMESTIC MEAT

2 large green bell peppers

1 large red bell pepper

2 large yellow onions

2 carrots

3 ounces olive oil

7 ounces pineapple chunks

7 ounces sliced mushrooms

1 pound raw meat, such as duck, chicken, turkey, pheasant, venison, pork, etc.

28 ounces sweet-and-sour sauce, may need a couple of bottles

Core peppers. Cut onions and peppers into 1/2-inch wedges. Peel and thinly slice carrots. Lightly saute vegetables in olive oil so that they are still crispy, and drain with strainer.

Saute meat in some olive oil. Heat sweet-and-sour sauce. Do not bring to boil. When hot, add meat and veggies. Mix together well. Serve over steamed rice. Serves 4 to 6 people.

THE JOINT AND ITS OWNERS DIDN'T FORGET WHERE THEY CAME FROM.

Phil's is now run by Pete Polizzi, a former college football player who busts chops with the regulars. It is the kind of kidding that only good friends can get away with. It ends with the customer walking away with a portion ample enough to straighten out any ruffled feathers.

Pete took over from his father, Phil, who was born in America but grew up in Italy, only to return as a young man to work in the garment district in Saint Louis, among other jobs.

Pete's mother, Teresa, is from Sicily, so food was always a big deal. They always wanted to own a restaurant, where they could share the food that they loved, but the restaurant they ended up buying was The Stumble Inn—a 3-2 beer joint that also had an outdoor barbecue pit—back in 1961.

"They didn't want to lose any customers, so they kept the barbecue and added their Italian," Pete tells me.

"A couple of years ago, this old guy came in and told me he had many fond memories of being underage and throwing down Griesidiecks and smoking Luckies at the bar that used to be here."

Pete points. "That old bar is still here. It was just too heavy to move, so we just kind of expanded around it."

One of my rules is to shy away any place with an extensive menu. Something usually suffers, and more often than not, it's the barbecue. But Phil's is the exception to that rule. Worlds do collide, and they do come together quite nicely. The Italian mixes with the American; sprinkle in a little Mexican, and there you have it.

I got an order of ribs and he threw in a side of spaghetti and a tamale, with his signature marinara/barbecue sauce.

The couple at the next table told me that I really should try the pizza. "It's the best in town," they said. I thanked them for their endorsement, but they would not settle for a thank you. They actually gave me a slice! Midwestern hospitality at its finest. It truly is a slice of heaven on a thin crust.

PHIL'S ITALIAN SAUSAGE

5 pounds ground pork*

1 medium onion, grated

3 tablespoons ground black pepper

3 cloves fresh garlic, minced

2 tablespoons salt

3 tablespoons fennel seed

1 medium onion, grated

3 tablespoons parsley (fresh or dried)

Grind the pork. In a large bowl, mix the pork with all the other ingredients. Cover with plastic wrap and refrigerate for at least 2 hours to allow for marrying of the ingredients. Shape into patties or put through grinder with sausage link attachment using hog casings.

*It is recommended to get a pork shoulder or Boston butt with a moderate amount of marbling (fat) to keep the sausage moist.

"MODELING OR BARBECUE?"

Debbie Webb says from across the table. "Those were the choices Mamma B. gave me. I was in modeling school and loved it. I showed a lot of promise, and there were opportunities, but I knew that I had a sure thing here."

Mamma B. is in fact Debbie's mother, but everyone calls her Mamma B. She is the matriarch of Bridges Barbecue, which she rules with an iron skillet. She is loved by all. "She still comes around, goes fishing on the weekend at Lake Norman and gets her hair and nails fixed on Monday. Just don't bother calling her when Bob Barker is on," Debbie warns.

Debbie isn't quite so blunt with her own son and daughter, Chase and Natalie. "They're free to pursue whatever they want," Debbie tells me.

Of course, they are carrying on the family business.

Red Bridges, Debbie's father, was a cook in the army and learned from legendary barbecue master Warner Stamey. He bought Dedman's Barbecue in 1946, and renamed it when they moved uptown in '49. They eventually moved into their new building in '53.

A lot has changed around Bridges Barbecue Lodge. The Putt-Putt with its go-cart track and farmland across the street have long been replaced by the Shelby Mall. But almost nothing has changed at Bridges. The building, with its neon sign, is classic Googie-style roadside Americana architecture.

"I tried to get her to change it, but now, I'm so glad she didn't listen to me," Natalie says from across the booth.

Debbie adds, "People want it to stay the way it is. The way they remember it when they were kids. My father planted those big oaks that line the parking lot when we first opened up. They are now nearly sixty years old and their roots are tearing up the parking lot. The word got out that I was thinking about cutting them down. Let me tell you, people started marching in here telling me I couldn't do that. 'I got my first kiss under those trees. Me and my sweetie used to picnic under those trees. Now we're grandparents. My first born was . . .'"

MAMMA B.'S DEVILED EGG SANDWICH

12 hard-boiled eggs, cooled

1/2 cup mayonnaise

6 tablespoons sweet pickle relish

1 teaspoon white pepper

1/3 teaspoon salt

Mash up the eggs and mix in all the ingredients. Cover and refrigerate for at least 2 hours. Put on your favorite bread and enjoy. Makes enough for 6 good-size sandwiches.

"ALWAYS HAD AT LEAST TWO JOBS, SOMETIMES THREE, AMONG THEM WORKING AT A BARBECUE JOINT,"

Wayne Monk tells me as he sips his morning coffee.

"That's when I got the idea of opening up my own place. I didn't have any money, so I borrowed $500 on my furniture and my brother-in-law, Sonny Honeycutt, put up the rest. We were equal partners. Three months into it, he decided barbecue wasn't for him. Not enough money.

"One thing he did that I never would have approved of was naming the place 'Honeymonks.' I showed up one day and the sign guy was putting it up. Some people still call it that and I changed the name forty years ago.

"I'm not what you might call a good cook," Wayne proclaims with the satisfaction of a man who knows that you don't believe him. "No, really, I'm a manager, a people person. I come in here real early and make sure everything's running smoothly.

"At any one time we usually have about fifteen family members working here, give or take a couple. They might leave, but they always come back." It only makes sense that Ricky Monk has taken over the day to day management duties. Ricky does share his father's personable approach, but he is equally at home in the kitchen.

"I wanted to go to Wake Forest, but wasn't a great student. I ended up at Davidson County Community

College, and was talking to a business professor about barbecue when I realized just how great I had it. I just love managing this place. Over the years I have come across a lot of people who say that they would like to own a barbecue place. I let them come over here and follow me around. Most decide to do other things."

Among the family and extended family is Ricky's son, Nathan. "He's in college, but he's always around here doing something. Mostly curb hopping, but helping out wherever he's needed. Just like me," Ricky says.

NOT EXACTLY
THEIR
COLESLAW
(BUT CLOSE)

1 large head cabbage

1/2 cup 40-grain vinegar (less acidic than apple cider vinegar)

1/4 cup sugar

1/2 cup ketchup

1/2 teaspoon salt

1 teaspoon ground black pepper

Core and shred cabbage (should have 5–6 cups). Whisk vinegar, sugar, ketchup, salt and pepper. In a bowl, mix with cabbage and refrigerate for at least 2 hours before serving.

"I WANNA DANCE WITH MY SHORT SUGAR!"

The juke box was playing in the grill where Eldridge Overby was working when his girlfriend walked in and made that now famous proclamation.

"The nickname stuck," David Wilson tells me with a bittersweet smile.

Several years later, Eldridge and his brothers Johnny and Clyde decided that they would build and operate a grill of their own. Unfortunately, Eldridge was killed in an auto accident while the restaurant was under construction.

The Overby brothers persevered with their dream, and when it opened up in November of 1949, they gave it the distinctive name in honor of their beloved brother.

David married into the Overby family in 1966, just out of UNC Chapel Hill with a degree in English. Over the course of a dozen years, he worked as a purchasing agent of machinery in the then-burgeoning textile industry.

"I would help out periodically during that time and realized what an important part of the community Short Sugar's is."

Today, Short Sugar's is known primarily as a barbecue restaurant, which it has been for over half a century, but its roots are unmistakably small town *American Graffiti* drive-in, circa 1950s, which fare it still serves. It was the focal point for the Reidsville kids cruising the strip on Saturday night.

David says, "I overhear grandfathers with their grandchildren, pointing to a spot in our parking lot, saying, 'Over there, that's where I first laid eyes on your grandma.'

"There is this one

couple. They would arrive at the same time. Sit at the same booth. Order the same meal. She would take the top off her sandwich and sprinkle on a little hot sauce. Just like clockwork every Saturday night. Only on this one occasion something caught her eye. Right next to the pickle on a big bed of barbecue was an engagement ring. So when the opportunity availed itself to carry on this place, how on earth could I possibly say no?"

"THIS IS NOT A JOB. IT'S A WAY OF LIFE.

We are very proud of that," Bruce Jones tells me as he tends to the customers who are lined up through the back door. "It takes fifteen hours to fully cook. We don't use the junk, but if it's on the hog, it's in our barbecue."

A lot might go into their barbecue, but the question remains: "How much?"

Except for the addition of coleslaw sometime along the way, a heap of barbecue with a slab of their cornbread is exactly how Skilton Dennis sold it off the back of a horse-drawn wagon in the mid-1830s at the Eureka Baptist Bible College. That is said to be the first time barbecue was sold in North Carolina.

Bruce finishes up with the lunch crowd and leaves for his other calling—as an ordained Freewill Baptist minister.

Bruce and his cousin Jeff own the place. Jeff did a little bit of everything before buying out his father's share in 1990. Like his cousin, he has been around barbecue his entire life. Even today, he lives in the house he grew up in, which is directly across the street.

Today, the future looks bright for the Skylight. Bruce's son Samuel, a seventh-generation practitioner of the art, has officially signed on.

"As a kid, I used to hate this," says Samuel. "Now I love it. This is my legacy. I was fifteen hours short of finishing at East Carolina when Grandpa's health started to fail. He worked twelve hours a day, six days a week until he was seventy-five. The family pull was just too much."

Some time ago, somebody hung the moniker "Barbecue Capital of the World" on Ayden, and though there are several cities that will challenge the title, the Skylight has been all too happy to promote it: the Skylight proudly wears

a replica of the capitol's rotunda on their roof.

Cooking barbecue the old-fashioned way—or, as Samuel puts it, the only way—is, sadly, a dying art. Modern gas smokers have taken most of the hands-on labor out of a labor-intensive venture, but it is the city ordinances prohibiting large open fires within city limits that have really dampened the coals of the traditional barbecue process.

"We were told that if we shut down during our remodeling in 1984, we could not re-open and cook this way [whole hog over an open pit]. To get around that, we remodeled the left side and then the right, remaining open all the while," Samuel proudly boasts.

BAR-B-QUE PRICES		
SANDWICH		2 50
TRAYS	SMALL	3 25
	MEDIUM	3.75
	LARGE	4 25
POUND		7 75
POUND	JUST B-B-Q	6 75
ALL ORDERS with SLAW and BREAD		
ALL PRICES TAX INCLUDED		
NO CHECKS		

NOT EXACTLY THE SKYLIGHT'S CORNBREAD

1-1/2 cups yellow cornmeal

3/4 cup flour

3 tablespoons sugar

1 tablespoon baking powder

1 teaspoon salt

2 large eggs

1-1/2 cups milk or buttermilk

1/4 cup shortening (melted)

Preheat oven to 400 degrees.

Combine dry ingredients (cornmeal, flour, sugar, baking powder, salt) and mix well.

Combine wet ingredients (eggs, milk/buttermilk, melted shortening) and mix well.

Combine wet and dry ingredients. Bake for 30 minutes in a well greased, 12-inch black skillet.

"THE MAN AT THE EMPLOYMENT OFFICE HAD TWO JOB OFFERS,"

Wilber Shirley tells me as he looks across the dining room. "One, a clerk at the Western Auto. The other, at Griffin's Barbecue.

"I went to work for Mr. Griffin in 1949 and except for a year of combat in Korea, I stayed with him until 1963.

"I probably would never have left Mr. Griffin's, but a friend kept after me about starting our own place. He eventually convinced me, put up the money and in 1963 we opened up Highway 70 Barbecue. Six months later he decided the barbecue business was not for him, and that's how Wilber's was born.

"That just goes to show, if you don't love what you do, don't do it. A barbecue joint is a lot like a newborn baby every day. You always have to be here to attend to it. I'm seventy-five and I'm still coming to work. I'm a blessed man.

"Looking back, the best part of all of this is being in a position to help people out. We had a boy from a broken home work here. We helped him go to college. After he graduated, he came back to town to teach school. He recently retired as a principal. To this day he comes back to help us out every weekend."

Wilber's is almost as much an intimate den as it is a barbecue joint. You can really get a good idea of what the man is all about just by looking at the knotty pine walls. There is the Democratic Party memorabilia, not the least of which is a large portrait of Franklin Roosevelt. There is even a letter of accommodation from the Party.

"When Bill Clinton was running for president the first time, he stopped by here. I have never seen anyone quite like him. We've had a lot of politicians come through and work a floor, but he spent almost as much time back in the kitchen talking with the cooks and waitresses. He really is a man of the people."

You can't miss the framed pictures and uniforms from all the branches of the United States Armed Forces. Wilber is a proud veteran, having put in a year of combat duty in Korea.

On the lighter side, Wilber is very active member of the North Carolina State University Wolfpack Club. "We used to travel to the ACC tournament every year. I sent my daughters there, and I don't think they attended one basketball game. Go figure."

EASTERN CAROLINA
VINEGAR–BASED
SAUCE
(SIMILAR TO WILBER'S)

1 quart apple cider vinegar

1 pint water

1/2 cup finely ground cayenne pepper

1/4 cup crushed cayenne pepper

1 tablespoon black pepper

1 tablespoon salt

2 tablespoons paprika

1 teaspoon dried mustard (optional for heat)

Combine all ingredients in a saucepan and bring to a boil. Once boiling, reduce heat and simmer for 30 minutes. It is ready to use. You might mix a little with your pork or chicken, but have it on the table so individuals can add to their tastes.

"LIFE'S TOO SHORT TO BE UNHAPPY. DO WHAT WILL MAKE YOU HAPPY."

That's what Jeanne Smith told her son, Charles.

"As I was walking through a field on Langston University's campus, it was then, I finally understood what she was talking about. 'Follow your dream!'" Charles proclaimed.

Momma was obviously right. A happier, more boisterous man you will not find. Rumbling around the joint, helping out his employees by jumping in wherever he sees a need. He greets everyone there like a friend. I suspect most are.

"Everyone gets a free slice of cake at Leo's. I can't tell you exactly when this tradition started, but one day someone 'suggested' putting a dessert on the menu. Dad and grandma concocted the strawberry-banana cake. We've been handing it out ever since."

W. Leo Smith opened his place in 1974. He learned the craft from his Uncle Ben, who had a joint in Tulsa. Over thirty years later, it still resembles the Sinclair gas station from which it sprung.

"I remember when we first opened. I was ten years old and I just knew this was what I wanted to do with my life," Charles states. "We didn't have nothing back then. Not even a cash register. We used a cigar box. We built everything. We laid down the floors, dropped the ceiling, built the pit."

"'The only way is the right way, and the right way is Leo's way!' my daddy would shout. Dad was tough. He would say, 'Shut up. Just look and learn.' The only time he let me ask questions and respected me as an equal was when I opened up my own place, which I did in '89." Charles appropriately named it Leo & Son's.

That venture didn't work out for Charles, but he never lost his passion. He sold barbecue out of a truck for a few years. "I would park it in front of Byron's Liquor Store during the week and take it from beauty shop to barber shop on the weekend. I was a one-man-band-rib-stand," Charles says.

Then, on October 14, 1997, the third anniversary of Leo's death, Leo's B-B-Q caught fire. The family was going to sell the land and what was left.

"I was not going to let that happen. I loved that place too much. It meant too much to the community and the people who worked there, so I parked the truck and took it upon myself to re-open."

Leo would have been proud.

CHARLES SMITH OF LEO'S B-B-Q'S FAVE CHICKEN

any amount of chicken

3 parts black pepper

1 part Lawry's seasoned salt

butter

1 lemon

Preheat oven or grill to 375 degrees. Season chicken with pepper and salt. Let stand in refrigerator 4 to 6 hours. Place chicken on shallow pan. Put pats of butter in each corner and cook for 1 hour, or until internal temperature of chicken is 180 degrees. Be sure to flip chicken at least two or three times. Once finished, squeeze fresh lemon juice on top.

"YOU'RE GOING TO MAKE IT. YOU'RE NOT LAZY."

That's what barbecue legend Alonzo "Slick" Smith told Bob Newton when he divulged that he was thinking of opening up his own place in town.

Bob was working for Slick at the time and had been a pitmaster at other barbecue joints around Muskogee. Yes, that's Muskogee, Oklahoma, USA.

"Slick was very encouraging. He was not afraid of competition, because he had no competition. He was the best," Bob says with reverence in his voice.

Slick died a few years ago, but thankfully, Bob carries on for him.

Bob is truly a humble man, and no barbecue lightweight. He also has quite a reputation on his own for barbecue. He literally had a cottage industry going on at home. People would bring him meat that he would smoke in his backyard on pits that he built.

"I believe that if you can't design your own pit, you can't cook. Most people just don't know the size and amount of meat to put on a pit," Bob states.

He is very proud of his mobile pits, which he takes on catering jobs and festivals. They work out especially well for him because of his cooking process.

"First I precook my meats. Then I cool them down by freezing them. Then I finish smoking. Cooling them down seasons the meat. You got to cool it down. I don't run out of meat this way, and I always have fresh barbecue on hand."

Bob is helped by his brother Eugene, upon whom the barbecue gods have bestowed the gift of knowing what you are going to order when you walk in the door.

Ronnie, Bob's younger brother, operates the family construction business. Together, they literally built their business from the

ground up. A low-lying brick and stone structure, it is very clean and efficient, and the envy of any restaurant.

The Newtons have several plots of land around town, which they use to grow most of their vegetables. In fact, next to the restaurant is the sweet potato patch that supplies the key ingredient for the famous pies that Eugene's wife, Patricia, makes on a daily basis.

All of this is done under the watchful eye of Bob's wife, Frankie. She makes sure every penny adds up. For all that the Newtons put in, you will more than get your money's worth.

Of course the children and grandchildren help out, too, but it gets better. Call him a family pet or a mascot, Big Cat hangs out on the front stoop, and when he is not busy greeting customers, he patrols the sweet potato patch and wood pile. The pay might be lousy, but as the old saying goes, you just can't beat the benefits.

PATRICIA
Sweet Potato Pie Queen

SMOKEHOUSE BOB'S
PATRICIA NEWTON'S
SWEET POTATO PIE

2 cups sugar

3 cups cooked, mashed sweet
   potatoes (about 4 large)

2 large eggs

2 teaspoons cinnamon

2 teaspoons allspice

2 teaspoons nutmeg

1 teaspoon lemon flavoring

1 teaspoon coconut flavoring

2 cups evaporated milk

Preheat oven to 350 degrees.

Mash sweet potatoes. Mix all ingredients together well. Pour into a prepared pie crust and bake 1 hour.

Wild Horse Mountain Bar-B-Q
HC 61 Box 404 • Sallisaw, OK 74955 • (918) 775-9960

"MY DAD WAS A CHARACTER."

"Crusty" was the most common description Bill Holman heard regarding his father.

"But you always knew where you stood with him. He would go about things his own way and didn't much care for outside help," Bill says.

"I remember as a kid I would offer up a suggestion and he'd shoot it down. I was stubborn and would push it. He would just grit his cigar and say in disgust, 'See if *you* can make it work.' He would be right most of the time, but I snuck in a couple of victories every once in a while."

Hubert and Betty, Bill's parents, were from Sallisaw—the same Oklahoma town Pretty Boy Floyd came from. "He's either an outlaw or a hero, depending on who you ask."

"I was six years old when we moved to Oklahoma. Dad left his job in Southern California with

Wham-O, you know, the Hula Hoop, Frisbee, Slip 'n' Slide company. We got all the rejects. One thing that I remember was this wind-up bird. It didn't work very well. It just knocked over lamps and broke things," Bill says with a laugh.

Hubert had his fill of California and brought his family back home to Sallisaw in 1965. They bought a house on the outskirts of town.

"We were near the Robert S. Kerr Dam and just started selling sandwiches to the workers. We had a Dairy Dip type place, but things really took off when we started selling barbecue."

Over the years, their reputation spread.

"Dad never believed in advertising, at least not the kind that you paid for. It's all word of mouth. One time the TV show *CBS Sunday Morning* came by and featured us. They flew into the little airport down the road and asked about getting a taxi to take them to the Wild Horse. The guy working at the airport said, 'It's just over the hill,' and threw them the keys to his truck. One of the CBS guys said, 'Where we come from they call that carjacking.'"

Hubert worked the barbecue until his health wouldn't allow it. He died in 1999. Betty still helps out some. Bill left his job making air pumps at Borg Warner and joined his brother Dale, who is retired from the Air Force, in taking over the barbecue. Both of the brothers' children help out as well.

"I guess you can say dad brought us all together."

"WHEN YOU GET YOUR OWN PLACE, DO IT YOUR WAY, BUT YOU'RE AT MINE."

That's what James Freeman Sr. told James Jr. whenever he made a helpful "suggestion."

James Sr. learned how to slow-cook hogs in an open pit from his grandfather. This tradition is now carried on by his son.

"I spent thirty-five years as an understudy. I came around to his way of thinking and I do it just like him."

James Jr. is a very personable guy. He greets all the regulars like family, and if a first-timer finds his way here, James Jr. will introduce himself and offer a rib or some hash to sample.

The backbone of their business is the loyal regulars. "We've got one guy, Joe, who comes in twice a day, sometimes three."

It goes without saying that James knows his way around smoke and fire. When he isn't the 'cue master, he is also a battalion chief with the local fire department.

"I was always hanging around here, but I got real serious when I was fifteen. I needed money to get a car. I eventually scraped together $500 to get a '66 VW Beetle. I made every dime right here!"

Freeman's is just across the river from Augusta and right on the way to Hilton Head Island. "A lot of people plan to stop here on their way. Over the years, we get to know the semi-regulars.

"We make our own charcoal here, and that is a secret my father perfected. It allows us to cook the hogs slow, slow, slow. It takes about twenty-four hours to cook a whole hog. We turn it once during that time. I can tell exactly when to turn it from the smell that the grease gives off when it hits the coals."

James is assisted by his wife, Christine, and their daughter Christa, a recent graduate of Spelman College. Christa is currently applying to law school. She comes back on weekends from Atlanta.

Freeman's is only open Thursday through Saturday, but it's all hands on deck during one particular week in April. That's when the eyes of the world cast their gaze firmly upon Augusta National Country Club, a couple of miles down the road, which hosts The Masters Golf Tournament.

"IF YOU GOTTA MAKE A LIVING DOING SOMETHING, I RECKON I'VE HAD A PRETTY GOOD GO OF IT,"

Jerry Hite tells me as he tends to his woodpile. Every other barbecue joint measures their output in terms of meat, be it in pounds, shoulders, hams, whatever. It would be very easy for Jerry to quantify his output in hogs, since he smokes the whole hog, but it is obvious his affinity is for the quality of his wood.

"A friend clears lots and brings us the hickory in thirty-foot sections. We cut them up exactly the way we like. On an average day, we will use two cords. Labor day, five. Fourth of July, ten.

"We're only open for business two days a week, but the rest of the time we're picking up supplies and ingredients. I'd rather pick them up. That way I can pick the best. It beats taking what they deliver."

There are also other advantages. "If I hear that the fish are biting, I'm out on the lake," Jerry notes.

"My father, John Sr., was a farmer, and occasionally he would cook a pig and sell the barbecue by the side of the road. He knew he had something, so he officially opened Hite's Barbecue in 1957, and I helped him out. I guess I just don't know any better. I freeze in the winter and burn up in the summer, but it's all I've ever done."

Hite's is strictly a take-out business. There are no seats inside or even a picnic bench outside. They sell pork for you to take home and cook yourself, but don't let that dissuade you from stopping by. I have found their barbecue sandwiches quite portable.

Brenda, Jerry's wife, came aboard when they bought out John Sr. in 1968. She left her job with R. L. Bryan Company, an office supply and equipment outfit that also recovered schoolbooks.

Despite being forced to rebuild due to a fire on the day before the nation's bicentennial, not much has changed. However, they do have a lot more help today. Jerry and Brenda's children (Bubba, David and Angie) are maintaining the family traditions, running a barbecue joint when not out fishing.

BRENDA HITE'S TIP ON COOKING WITH FATBACK

Fatback gives vegetables a smoky flavor and a creamy texture. It is especially good on any type of bean or green vegetable.

Slice off some fatback and fry in a pan until brown and crispy. The grease will render out. You can add a little bit of meat, but use 1 teaspoon of drippings per cup of vegetables.

"WE'RE LIKE TRAVELING BACK TO AN EARLIER TIME."

"My family was farmers. We raised hogs and row crops," Bill Sweatman tells me as he pats his brow with a towel draped on his shoulder. He is concentrating on the dozens of ingredients that go into the 80-gallon pot where his legendary hash is concocted.

Bill, a big man with an even bigger voice, can be heard echoing around the cinder-block structure where they smoke and dress the hogs. He took over the hash duty from his father, Elliott, after he passed away in 2001. "I put in my twenty-six years as a long haul trucker. I was ready to come back home, to stay.

"We used to have a big family picnic for grand-daddy every year. My dad and uncle would do up a whole hog. Smoke it in a pit. Not much different than what we are serving here today. Word spread, and it seemed like just about every weekend they were doing some function. People were encouraging them to do this full time."

By the mid 1970s things had gotten so bad for the small family farmer that the Sweatmans did finally give in and heed that advice. They got some land with a farmhouse that looks every day of its 120 years. It is still a work in progress today. Just grab a plate, fill it up, find a place to sit and make yourself right at home. Eat 'til your heart's content. You can always go back as many times as you want.

A portrait of the founders, Bud and Margie, graces the bead-board walls, but the reigns have long been passed on to their daughters Judy, Patricia and Susan. They manage the kitchen, prepare the sides, stock the buffet, keep the kids in line and needle each other like only sisters can. After all, this *is* a family gathering.

SOUTH CAROLINA MUSTARD–BASED BARBECUE SAUCE

I got this off the South Carolina Dining website. They say that this one can be traced back to German settlers of the eighteenth century. (Incidentally, I didn't know that French's mustard had been around that long.)

2 cups yellow mustard (one 20-ounce bottle of French's mustard should do the trick)

4 ounces beer (less for thicker sauce)

1/4 cup apple cider vinegar

4 tablespoons brown sugar

1/4 cup tomato puree

1/2 tablespoon cayenne pepper

1/2 tablespoon fresh cracked black pepper

1/2 tablespoon garlic powder

1 teaspoon Worcestershire sauce

1 teaspoon salt

In a saucepan, heat all ingredients over medium heat and mix well. Cook until sauce just begins to thicken. Serve cool or warm. The sauce will last a good couple of months in the refrigerator. Makes about 3 cups.

SOUTH CAROLINA HASH

This recipe is from Sadler Taylor, Chief Curator of Folklife Research at the McKissick Museum at the University of South Carolina in Columbia. He said that this is a good basic recipe. He also noted that it is also hard to get an exact break down of the amounts, because it varies so much from batch to batch. If your batch happens to be a little thick (my wooden mixing spoon was able to stand upright), add a little extra tomato sauce or water.

2 medium yellow onions, chopped

1 (28-ounce) can potatoes, chopped

1 (29-ounce) can tomato sauce

5 ounces Heinz 57 sauce

2 teaspoons Worcestershire sauce

2-1/2 ounces Texas Pete hot sauce

1/2 tablespoon salt

1/2 tablespoon black pepper

1 tablespoon butter

3 pounds beef (or pork or both)

In a 4-quart pot over high heat, mix all ingredients together except the meat; cover and bring to a boil. Reduce heat to a simmer and cover for about 2 hours; stirring occasionally so that it doesn't burn on the bottom of the pot.

Meanwhile cook the meat according to your preference, just make sure that it is fully cooked. When done, finely chop it up (a food processor works great for this). Stir the meat into the pot for the last 10 minutes of cooking. This is usually made in large batches and also freezes well. Serve over rice, grits or with some white bread.

"WE HAVE SEATING TO ACCOMMODATE 10,000,"

Andy Garner says with a sly smile. Katy just rolls her eyes. She's heard that one a time or two.

Theirs is a living, breathing contradiction: an unassuming take-out window off a screened-in porch with two large picnic tables, sharing a parking lot with, of all places, the McDonalds next door.

"It works out real good for both of us," Katy says. "The kids get their Happy Meals™, and the parents come over here and get a sandwich."

But what really makes this location special is that just across the street is the Parthenon at Centennial Park.

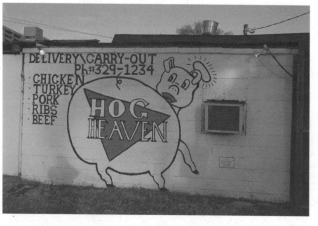

Andy and Katy bought their little slice of heaven in 1989, from the guy who beat them to it a few months earlier. "He called us to ask if we still wanted it. We ended up being the fourth owners in three years," Andy says. "It was just meant to be," Katy adds.

Andy and Katy met a few years earlier when they were both students at Middle Tennessee State University. Katy was a broadcast journalism major and Andy majored in, as he puts it, "partying." When you think about it, that is the perfect prerequisite for owning a barbecue joint.

Prior to acquiring Hog Heaven, Andy had worked at a string of jobs, often a couple at a time. He worked in and managed restaurants. Helped out his brother in the printing business. He even sold cars for a while, then quit because, as he puts it, "It was like stealing from the poor and giving to the rich."

When they got that call, Katy was pregnant with their first child, Richard. She kept her job as a makeup artist at a local department store. "We kept the job. We needed the insurance. Our second, Christopher, was on the credit card.

"We used to put Richard in a box," Andy chuckles. "People would hear rumbling coming from the box. They thought there was a puppy rumbling around in there, and when they asked to take a look, we'd oblige them and lift little Richard up. It would really freak them out."

Today, Richard and Christopher have grown into strapping lads, and can often be found helping out their parents at the joint. Just grab a bag full, park yourself under a big shady tree, and find out for yourself what they mean by "Hog Heaven."

KATY GARNER'S HOG HEAVEN FRUIT COBBLER

1-1/2 pounds frozen peaches or blackberries

3 cups sugar, divided

2 cups flour

2 teaspoons baking powder

1/2 teaspoon salt

6 tablespoons butter

1 cup milk

3 ounces butter, melted

Preheat oven to 375 degrees.

Weigh 1-1/2 pounds frozen peaches, blackberries or any other fruit you desire into container. You can use fresh fruit if you can get it. Pour 1/2 cup sugar over fruit, thaw in microwave or overnight in refrigerator. Mix dry ingredients with 2 cups sugar. Add melted butter and milk; blend well. Butter an 8 x 8-inch metal pan and pour in batter; cover with fruit. Sprinkle remaining sugar over fruit and dot with additional butter. Bake for 45 minutes, or until golden brown and firm. Makes about 12 servings.

"ISN'T GOD FUNNY?"

Flora Payne says with a chuckle. "This was my husband and mother-in-law's idea, *not* mine. I'm just left."

Payne's Barbecue on Lamar opened for business in 1972. It is a converted gas station, just down the street from its original location. Flora runs it with help from Earl Parker, who has been there eighteen years. They keep busy. To say it is sparsely appointed would be an understatement. "We think about fixing it up, but we have never got around to it."

Their menu is propped up on the floor in the corner. You go to a long window that says "Place Order Here" on the left and "Pay Here" on the right. From the window you can see the brick pit and an old Norge stove.

Turn around and the dining area is a mass of mismatched tables and chairs. The service bay doors from its gas station days are now windows, and they are covered with large bamboo roll shades. There are a couple of artificial trees. If they were real, they would have choked on hickory smoke a long time ago. There are several small metal found-object sculptures donated by an appreciative customer.

There is also an award plaque from an obscure

publication dated 1988, and that is about it. Flora is too modest to brag about herself. That is best left to her customers. Standing in line, a pair of local businessmen told me that both Memphis food critics independently rated hers number one. The *New York Times* anointed her "First Lady of Memphis Barbecue."

The future is looking bright for Payne's. Daughter Candace is taking a more active roll. "Mom was a little worried, but I never thought of anything else," she tells me.

"My dad passed when I was eleven, so I kind of grew up here. I always enjoyed helping out and working alongside my mom and grandmother."

Just a suggestion: When you do eventually take over, please, please don't change a thing.

OLD-FASHIONED CORNBREAD
(NOT ON THEIR MENU)

3/4 cup flour

1 teaspoon salt

3 teaspoons fresh baking powder

3 teaspoons sugar

1-1/2 cups yellow cornmeal

2 large eggs

1-1/2 cups milk or buttermilk

1/4 cup shortening (melted)

Combine dry ingredients and mix well. Combine wet ingredients and mix well. Combine wet and dry ingredients. Bake at 400 degrees in a greased 12-inch black iron skillet for about 30 to 40 minutes, or until a toothpick inserted in the center comes out clean.

I MAKE A CONCERTED EFFORT NOT

to highlight joints that are close in proximity, and especially if they have the same name, but for the Payne's of Memphis, I will make an exception.

Sandra Payne's story is similar to that of her sister-in-law, Flora. It was her husband, Lomas, who followed his brother and mother into the barbecue business. Sometime after the original Payne's on Lamar moved to its current location, Lomas took over the old location in·1981. They have since relocated to their current loacation on Elvis Presley Boulevard.

Though both Paynes are unpretentious, the simple menus have evolved differently. In addition to barbecue, they have rib tips, hot links, and smoked sausage. They also open and close later.

Lomas is now unable to work, and so the management of the operation is in the very capable hands of his wife, Sandra. She comes straight from her job as a third grade teacher, which she has been doing at the same school for over 35 years.

"I'm teaching my children's children," she proudly states. "I have no plans on retiring any time soon. I love what I'm doing too much, and this is a nice change of pace."

The decision of relocating to Elvis Presley Boulevard was a conscience decision Sandra says.

"We wanted to get the tourists who flock to Graceland a couple of miles down the road. I met Elvis before he was famous. He and a friend stopped by the Memphis Blood Center where my mother worked. My friend said, 'You just watch, he is going to make it big someday.' I remember him as a very sweet and shy young man."

Graceland is six lights south, but the recently opened Stax Museum of American Soul Music is just around the corner on McLemore Avenue, and is a definite must see. You should make a point to see the very underrated Sun Studio Tour, just a couple miles north.

Dear God,
  So far today I have done alright. I haven't gossiped or lost my temper. I haven't been greedy, grumpy, nasty, selfish or over indulgent. But in

a few minutes, God, I'm going to get out of bed, and from then on I'm going to need a lot more help.

"SON, YOU KNOW WHAT TO DO."

"I've been the best I can, and you can be better." That's what Mr. Scott told Ricky Parker in the spring of 1989. The Scotts took a liking to him when they spotted him working at Morgan's Service Station. Ricky was fourteen years old.

"Mr. Scott was a no-nonsense old-fashioned sort of man," Ricky says. "He liked that I didn't grow my hair out long as was the style back then. He asked about me and found out I was working three jobs and going to school. He introduced himself and told me I now had only one job."

Ricky was a hard worker. That was obvious, something a barbecue man could easily spot. After all Early Scott started selling barbecue by the side

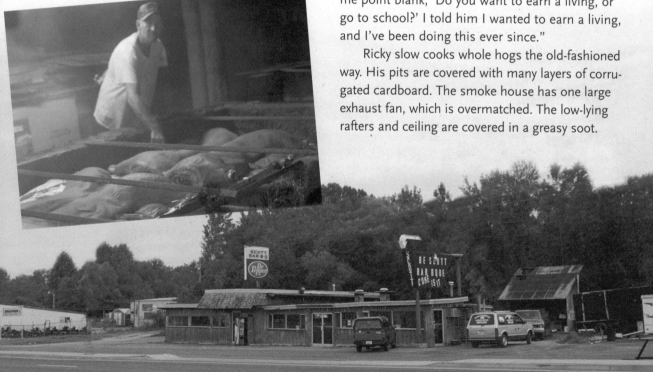

of the road, with only 18 dollars to his name. What wasn't so obvious was the terrible situation Ricky faced at home.

"On one particular night I came home and saw my father beating on my mother. I took a baseball bat to him. He threw me out of the house. Told me I didn't live there anymore. The Scotts adopted me the next day."

Ricky had already been working for the Scotts for two years. They didn't have any children, and besides, they already treated him like their own.

"Mr. Scott used to check me out of school at 11:00 and return me at 1:00 every day to help out during the lunch rush. I would work before and after school, too. When I was a senior, he asked me point blank, 'Do you want to earn a living, or go to school?' I told him I wanted to earn a living, and I've been doing this ever since."

Ricky slow cooks whole hogs the old-fashioned way. His pits are covered with many layers of corrugated cardboard. The smoke house has one large exhaust fan, which is overmatched. The low-lying rafters and ceiling are covered in a greasy soot.

"They won't insure me, but they can't shut me down neither. I'm grandfathered in."

Ricky's wife, Tina, is a nurse at the cardiac-cath unit of Jackson General. "I mess 'em up, she fixes 'em up," Ricky tells between puffs from his Swisher Sweet.

"She helps out as do our four kids. I hope that some day I can throw one of them the keys."

RICKY PARKER'S BBQ HOT SAUCE

They do this by sight, and it's not written down, so it's always a little different.

2 tablespoons sugar

1 tablespoon black pepper

3/4 teaspoon cayenne pepper

pinch salt

8 ounces apple cider vinegar

Mix all dry ingredients in an empty bottle, then pour in half the vinegar. Shake well, then add the rest of the vinegar and shake again. If too hot for your taste, add sugar or vinegar to dilute. You can also start over and cut back on the pepper.

"I CAN'T AFFORD TO BUY THIS,"

Charlie Robertson told the current owner of Three Little Pigs Bar-B-Q back in 1989.

Charlie was a bread man driving for the Colonial Baking Company at the time, and this was one of the stops on his route.

Three Little Pigs Bar-B-Q had been around since 1964. In the early days, it was a Loeb's Barbecue, a local chain founded by the brother of the mayor of Memphis. Loeb's sold out in 1981, and the restaurant had been through a series of owners and name changes by the time Charlie found it on his route.

"He was a retired banker with a military back-ground. He had no idea of what he had got him-self into. The place was doing poorly and he wanted out in the worst way."

Charlie, however, knew exactly what he was getting into. Before he became a bread man, he had managed several fast food restaurants, including Dairy Queen, Whataburger and Arthur Treacher's Fish & Chips.

"I saw potential and was confident that I could make it work, but I just didn't have the money, but he told me not to worry. He could 'fix it.' After all, he was a retired banker.

"My wife, Juvenia, was very supportive, and

my three sons were a great help, but we were really fortunate to have had Helen McClendon. She pretty much came with the building, sort of a fixture. She had been here almost since Loeb's opened up. Owners had come and gone, but she had been the one constant. She could do it all. I don't think that I could have pulled it off without her."

These days, age and health are catching up with Helen, but she still comes in and makes their signature beans and sauce.

Since Charlie took over, he has been able to realize that potential that he saw. "We've made some improvements to the building. It used to be so smoky in here. These used to be glass walls with no insulation. You would burn up in the summer and freeze in the winter."

Three Little Pigs is a freestanding building in a shopping-center parking lot. It has really been embraced by the neighborhood, as evidenced by the display racks in the dining room. They are overflowing with pig figurines.

"I don't buy them. People keep bringing them to me from all over the world. Now when someone brings me a new one, I have to take one down. I have several boxes of them in storage. I can't bring myself to throwing them out."

CHARLIE ROBERTSON'S THREE LITTLE PIGS

SLAW DRESSING

- 1 green cabbage
- 1 medium onion
- 1 cup mayonnaise
- 1 cup sweet pickle relish
- 4 tablespoons yellow mustard
- 1/3 cup sugar

Core and chop cabbage. Finely chop onion. Mix all ingredients. Allow to sit 2 to 3 hours in the refrigerator before enjoying.

"THIS STARTED OUT AS SOMETHING TO DO BETWEEN GETTING LAID OFF,"

Ron Janow tells me at the covered picnic tables along the side of his joint. He takes a sip of his favorite beverage.

"I worked for the Southern Pacific Railroad as a track laborer. The work was seasonal, which gave me a lot of downtime to do other things. I helped my dad. He was the Pearl Beer distributor for Colorado County. I also managed a country-rock band called 'South Fork.' You have to remember, this was the early '80s."

During one of Ron's layoffs, an old girlfriend from high school, Denice Austin, also found herself out of work. She had been laid off from Texas Instruments in Houston.

"Her family had a grocery store which had been in the family since the turn of the century, among other businesses around town. They sold a homemade sausage, which we started to smoke and sell on Saturdays."

Eagle Lake is an old town just west of Houston. It used to be on the main road, until I-10 bypassed them in the early 80s. They still are on a major truck route, which has kept the town afloat.

Things were going so well that Ron and Denice made it official, got married, expanded their barbecue operation, and moved to an old Texaco station that her parents owned. Over the years, they added on to the old gas station, and today they are open for business three and a half days per week, but they do so much catering, they often work seven.

"Between me and my wife, someone is always here. Our son and daughter help out. They're in high school and we're always taking them around

to some activity. They are real involved in the FFA. They started with rabbits and last year, our son was a grand champion in goats and our daughter, a grand champion in lambs."

When Ron is not at his joint or hauling kids around, he can be found recharging his battery on one of the nearby lakes or bays—fishing.

"I just love to hit the lake, but I miss my old fishing buddy, Jerry Fink. He got me into fishing and really helped me out big time. He also got me started in the corporate catering by landing me my first couple of clients."

DENICE JANOW'S
AUSTIN'S BBQ
MACARONI SALAD

1 (16-ounce) box macaroni

1 green bell pepper, finely minced

1 small yellow onion, finely minced

4 stalks celery, finely minced

1 cup mayonnaise

3/4 cup sweet pickle relish

2 tablespoons French salad dressing

2 tablespoons Italian dressing

2 teaspoons ground black pepper

1 teaspoon salt

Cook macaroni according to package directions; rinse and strain with cold water. Combine all ingredients and mix thoroughly. Let set in refrigerator for at least 2 hours.

"DON'T WORRY GIRL. I'LL BE HERE."

That's what Wylie Alexander told Shirley Bagley when she was thinking about buying the aptly named "Beans N Things."

Shirley was a residential real estate broker in Albuquerque, when her husband relocated to the Texas Panhandle. He had been eating at Beans N Things and knew the owner wanted to sell. He thought it would be something good for Shirley to do despite the fact that she had never had any restaurant experience.

As a real estate agent, one becomes well versed in the three rules necessary for the success of a commercial property, and they are as follows, in no particular order: location, location and location.

"This place was rundown, and on the wrong side of town," Shirley says. "There were vacant lots, bums and hookers everywhere, but it did have a good reputation and Wylie put me at ease. It was like I had known him all my life. He was going to be at his flower shop next door, and his brother lived in the house behind the place. And besides, I never back down from anything."

Fifteen years later, her place on the famous Route 66 is still doing great, and the neighborhood has drastically improved.

"Wylie still sticks his head in every day and always tells me I'm doing a fine job. That makes me feel good," Shirley tells me.

"I just love this place. I will never leave. My son Tim worked with me here. He recently died of a congenital heart defect. We had no idea. He was always playing tricks. Things just seem to move around here for no apparent reason. We just say, 'That must be Tim, again.'"

"I call this place Wylie's Museum. He was a World War II vet and he has a lot of that memorabilia displayed. He also nailed a craps table to the ceiling. It is rumored to be from

a raid when he was chief of police, but he denies it.

"People also bring in stuff. One day this old man came in and said that picture over there was his. I told him if he wanted to take it back, he could. He told me not today. He would come by every now and again and on one occasion he said, 'I decided that I like you. You can keep it.'"

BEANS N THINGS
HELLISH
RELISH

1/4 cup red bell peppers

1 tablespoon oil

2 cups jalapeños

Roast red peppers on an open fire or in pan with oil until the skin starts getting white, then turns brown. When brown, let cool for a minute; peel and chop. Roast jalapeños, peel and chop (if you want it hot, keep seeds).

Variation: This is an optional step for serious heat. Put in a few drops of habanero sauce or 1 habanero pepper, roasted and chopped.

Wylie

Tim

Note: Do not put in blender. Wear gloves (vinyl or latex). If oil gets on hands, wash immediately in apple cider vinegar to neutralize.

"I'M A BULLSHITTER,"

Lynn "Big O" Owens says with pride as he leans back on one of his dining room chairs. And that is exactly what he was doing with some of his soon-to-be-former coworkers at Texas Instruments in the spring of 1993—bullshitting.

"We had just been told that they were going to be closing the plant. I had been with them for eighteen years. We were talking about what we were going to do, and I said I was going to open up a tackle store down by the lake. Everybody laughed, and then I got to thinking it wasn't such a crazy idea.

I went to check it out, and sure enough all the good locations were already taken, so I found this old empty gas station that was on the main road, I leased it and opened up my convenience/tackle store.

"When they started construction on the highway there were only a couple of places around here for the road crew to eat. I wanted to get a piece of that action, so I started selling some pre-made barbecue out of a slow cooker. It sold well, but I knew that I could do a lot better. So I started to make my own real barbecue. It worked out real good.

"Then around about that time, the oil companies ran me and most of the independent mom and pops out of the gas business by forcing us to upgrade our tanks. It just would have cost too much. That's when I found this location and I have been expanding around it ever since."

Valera is just a dot on the map, and Big O's is a gathering place for the entire community.

"Kids just love my sign. 'He's getting poked in the butt.' I never get tired of hearing that."

The walls of his dining area are covered with the artwork of those appreciative kids.

Big O is still an avid fisherman. He is also a freelance journalist for various outdoor magazines and an occasional hunting and fishing columnist for the local *Coleman Chronicle*. He even sells fishing tackle in the room just off the dining area.

"You can get a barbecue with a side of nightcrawlers here," he says with a big grin.

"I get to concentrate on the barbecuing and fishing, and the bullshitting with the customers. My wife Trisha works in a bank. She handles the books. It works out pretty good."

BIG O'S FRIED TILAPIA

2 pounds fresh tilapia

3 pounds yellow cornmeal

1-1/2 cups flour

pinch of salt

pinch of pepper

oil (preferably cottonseed)

Slice the fish into small, even strips. This will allow the fish to cook evenly. The slices should not exceed 1-1/4 inches in thickness.

Put the cornmeal and flour into a double paper bag. Add a pinch of salt and pepper. Shake to mix thoroughly. Take half the fish and dump it into the bag. Fold the top of the bag and shake some more.

Heat the oil to 375 degrees. Pull fish from the bag and shake off excess mix. Place it in the fryer basket or pan. When done, salt immediately and let stand for at least 3 minutes before serving.

Always keep a shaker of Tony Chachere's Original Seasoning handy for a little extra spice. Serves 2 to 4 people—or one big ol' boy.

Note: It's better to fry small amounts of fish at a time. Once the fish floats, it's done. The fish should never be wet inside the crust.

"YOU'RE NOT GOING TO BELIEVE THIS, BUT I WON THIS PLACE IN A CARD GAME,"

says Buddy Ellis.

Like any good gambler, he told what sounded like a tall tale, but at the table, that was full of family and friends, who would chime in with an occasional, "Now, that's true."

"I was working for the highway department at the time. Along with some money I saved up from the army, I had enough to start this place.

"My dad and uncle had worked at a couple of barbecue places in the area. They would run the place during the week and I would help out on the weekend. We opened May 16, 1958. Our first day sales was $28.75. Needless to say, I didn't quit my day job."

Buddy Ellis did eventually quit his day job, and the City Market has grown and expanded several times over the decades. "I've got about seventeen-eighteen people working here now. I don't know what half of them do." His sons help out with the cattle, chicken, oil and rent business.

Buddy doesn't manage the market. That's left to Joe Capello. Joe started when he was eight. Buddy spotted him unloading watermelons. "It was about a hundred degrees and those melons were nearly the size of him. I figured pushing a broom was more his speed."

Growing up, Joe would live and go to school in the next town, but during the summer, he would live with the Ellises and work at City Market. Other than a hitch in Vietnam, City Market is the only place he has ever worked.

"When I got back, I got married and went to work. I was trying to figure out what I was going to do next, when Buddy told me to manage this place."

Joe wears a hard hat, but not as a result of an injury or accident.

"Buddy's mother, Delma, gave this to me about thirty-five years ago. She always looked out for me. I have had the lining replaced a few times over the years."

Buddy showed me around the place, pointing out campaign posters for the watermelon "Thump Queen."

"That one over there is my granddaughter. It'll be the worst thing for her to win it."

Spoken like a true gambler.

CITY MARKET'S COUNTRY-STYLE PORK SAUSAGE

10 pounds Boston butt

2 tablespoons black pepper

2 tablespoons salt

1 tablespoon red pepper

1/4 cup brown sugar

Cut the butt into chunks. Mix all ingredients together and grind twice; first using a coarse chile plate and then using a finer sausage plate. Stuff in pork casings or just make into patties.

"NOT MUCH HAS CHANGED AROUND HERE SINCE I BOUGHT THIS PLACE FROM MR. COOPER,"

Duard Dockal tells me in his storage room and office. "And that goes for this town too. I never thought I'd be doing this. My dad had a barbecue place here, and growing up, I worked there. He sold it and retired in 1962. Since then, it had several owners over the years, but it eventually closed down."

Duard never left the Mason area, but he did manage to do a little bit of everything from farming and ranching to working at an all-night truck stop before he realized that he was a barbecue lifer.

"We came to an agreement that I would buy this place from Mr. Cooper when he decided to retire. I put in six-and-a-half-years before he eventually did on January 1, 1983.

"I really enjoy over-hearing parents and grandparents telling their kids and grandkids that it's just like it was when they were their age."

Just walk up to the "Order Here" sign in front of the large pit. One of a team of young guys will cut you exactly as much as you want of whatever they have on the pit, usually brisket, chicken, pork, sausage or ribs—sometimes, even goat. In the check-out room they have sides and beverages. You can get it to go, take it to the air-conditioned dining room, or sit outside at the covered picnic area, where you can get a real appreciation for what exactly goes into making great barbecue.

When not serving customers, they are doing the hundreds of other things, not the least of which is the transformation of mesquite logs to coals. This process takes place in a quartered old oil-field butane tank, which stands about 10 feet tall. The smoldering hot coals are then carted, right in front of you, into the pit. This ain't no backyard operation.

DUARD DOCKAL'S BEANS

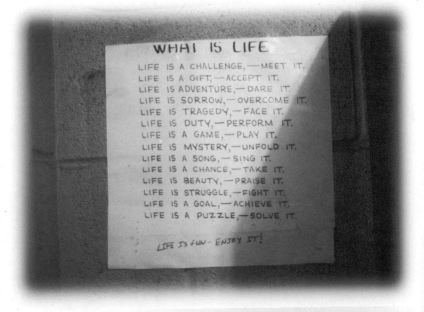

2 pounds pinto beans
  (soaked overnight)

1/2 cup chopped raw bacon

1 medium yellow onion, chopped

2 large jalapeños

1/2 cup ketchup

2 tablespoons salt

2 tablespoons garlic

1-1/3 tablespoons cilantro (dried or fresh diced)

2 teaspoons black pepper

2 teaspoons sugar

1/3 teaspoon baking soda

Cook all ingredients to a rolling boil, then simmer with lid on for about 3-1/2 to 4 hours, or until the beans are tender.

"I WAS YOUNG AND FOOLISH AND DIDN'T KNOW ANY BETTER,"

Charlotte Finch told me as she took a gulp of sweet tea. "I was an office manager at a debt collection company when I saw this place for sale, and knew I just had to do it."

What Charlotte saw was the F. Weigl Iron Works Foundry, located right in downtown Austin. The place was in terrible disrepair. It would have been easier just to bulldoze the place, as was the custom in 1978, but that was not an option. She made do with what remained, not only celebrating the building's history by naming it "Iron Works Barbecue," but displaying its former occupant's tools of the trade as well. The soul of the building is also evident in all the brands tattooed on any available wooden surface.

The only restaurant experience Charlotte had ever had was eating at one—that, and growing up on a ranch in Kerrville, Texas. "Being one of four-

teen children will teach you a lot about sharing and responsibility," she says.

"This has been a great learning experience from day one, and I'm still trying to figure it out. I remember when I was finally able to actually hire someone and I watched as she cut an onion. I didn't like the way she did it, but it got us where we needed to go, so I went with it. I'm not big on training people how to do things, as long as they get them done. Thankfully, I don't have to waste a lot of time training people."

As far as this joint goes, Charlotte likens it to a child that still hasn't quite grown up: "I feel like I'm almost there, but not there yet." Which probably explains why she hasn't sold this prime piece of downtown real estate, no matter how juicy the offer.

NOT QUITE THE IRON WORKS BARBECUE TEXAS CHILI

This chili is not found at the Iron Works. They have their own chili in the winter. You can find that recipe, and purchase the secret seasoning that the recipe requires, at www.ironworksbbq.com.

3 pounds coarse ground beef

1 pound fresh pork sausage

4 (28-ounce) cans stewed tomatoes

2 medium yellow onions, chopped

8 cloves garlic, chopped

3 tablespoons flour

2-1/2 ounces dark chili powder

2 tablespoons dark smoked Spanish paprika

2 tablespoons smoked chipotle pepper

4 tablespoons cumin powder

1 (6-ounce) can tomato paste

3 (16-ounce) cans beans (black, red, ranch, or pinto)

sliced jalapeño peppers to taste

salt to taste

Brown ground beef and pork sausage. Drain off grease. Add tomatoes, onion, garlic, and flour. Continue to saute with meat until onion turns opaque. Add other ingredients and simmer for 1 hour. Adjust to taste.

"HOW'S THE BRISKET TODAY, BOBBY?"

A man at the counter yells over to Bobby Mueller as he works at the chopping block. Not looking up, he hurls a piece of meat to that place in the front of the line.

"I'll have the brisket," the man tells the woman at the cash box.

It must be a routine they have. Asking Bobby Mueller "How's the brisket?" is like asking the Pope what religion he is.

The man tells me with a chuckle, "I've been coming here forever. I like to go sit over there by the business cards. If you look long and hard enough you'll find one of mine from the 1970s."

Louie Mueller came to Taylor from Collinsville, Illinois to open up a Safeway grocery store in the mid-1930s. He eventually opened up his own Red

& White grocery store in 1946. To make sure their meat was always fresh, he made sausage from the trimmings, and sold barbecue. He lasted in the grocery business until 1974.

"Dad had too big of a heart and gave too many people credit," says Bobby.

Growing up, Bobby always enjoyed helping out the family, but he didn't expect to make this his life's work. He went to Texas Christian University in Fort Worth to study business, followed by time in the service. Then he came back home and never left.

"I didn't plan on it; it just kind of happened," he tells me from one of the plywood tables.

Like so many things in life, plans just sort of happen. And if you do it well, hopefully you will get some recognition. If not, you take with you the satisfaction of knowing you did your best.

Bobby points to a table. "It was built by our handyman when we first moved here in 1951. It's exactly four-foot square. Eight people can sit here comfortably."

At that time some customers show up and Bobby excuses himself to serve them.

Upon closer inspection, the table is so simple—just a 4 x 8-foot sheet of plywood doubled over with trim and legs, and cured with half a century's worth of mesquite smoke.

Bobby's wife Trish remains. "He won't brag on himself, but we got the James Beard Award. We heard about him, but didn't know about his foundation. We found out just how prestigious it is. It was very exciting for us to go to the ceremony in New York to accept it."

BOBBY MUELLER'S POTATO SALAD

4 pounds russet potatoes

3 hard-boiled eggs, chopped

2-1/4 cups real mayonnaise

1-1/4 cups dill pickle relish

1-1/4 cups yellow mustard

3 tablespoons black pepper

3 stalks celery, chopped

Boil potatoes with skins on in covered pot until done, between 60–90 minutes. Allow potatoes to cool in refrigerator or by running or soaking in cold water. When cool, peel and dice into desired-size chunks. Mix and mash everything together with a potato masher for that creamy/lumpy texture. Refrigerate at least 1 hour to set before serving.

"I'VE SEEN A LOT OF BARBECUE JOINTS OPEN AND CLOSE 'ROUND HERE, ALONG WITH EVERYTHING ELSE,"

Lee Hammond tells me as he leans back in his chair.

When your joint is in Midland, your fortunes are tied to the oil industry.

"I had just retired from the Army in 1979. I was only thirty-eight. I joined when I was seventeen and was all set to go to Turkey as a civilian contractor for big bucks. I came home just to visit with my family in Odessa. They had a convenience store and deli. They sold barbecue and hot links, mostly to the junior high kids across the street.

"The big oil boom had just started and we expanded the place. My cousin Sam was the main cook, and he started to expand the place. Put in a steam table, and at lunch time, there was a line out the door. Money was flowing everywhere.

"My wife Jackie and I were high school sweethearts, and she didn't want to leave the area."

Lee never made it to Turkey. He opened up their first Midland location. They eventually had five in Midland and two in Odessa. Then the bust came.

"It was bad. Banks were going out of business. People were leaving the area in droves. We just tightened our belts. Ended up closing up joints. Today we just have the one here and Odessa.

Over the sound system there is blues playing.

"One of the joints we had going was real upscale. It had musical acts. We were on "the circuit." I would get calls from booking agents from all over the country, calling me up to place acts. They really liked it here. I even helped start the West Texas Blues Festival.

"I identify with the blues. People in this town really identify with the blues. I guess that is why I just love these people so much. I've seen them when they were little kids, and I have catered their weddings. I give them 100 percent and they give back.

"My wife and I have one son, who is in the seminary, but we have plenty of nieces and nephews to help out. I just hope one of them takes over someday."

SAM'S OLD–FASHIONED BEEF BRISKET STEW

4-1/2-pound beef brisket, cut into cubes

1/2 cup shortening

4 cups sliced carrots

2 cups chopped onions

4 cloves garlic, minced

10 cups cubed potatoes

2 cups chopped celery

2 teaspoons paprika

2 tablespoons Worcestershire sauce

2 tablespoons salt

1/4 teaspoon pepper

5 cups water, divided

1/2 cup flour

Brown brisket in a 12-quart Dutch oven with shortening. Combine browned meat with vegetables, paprika, Worcestershire sauce, salt, pepper and 4 cups water. Cook, covered, over medium heat for about 1 hour. Add flour and 1 more cup water to boiling stew mixture. Stir and cook until bubbly.

"THERE ARE TWO THINGS I WANT YOU TO REMEMBER. NEVER FORGET THE GOOD TIMES AND NEVER MAKE ME CRY."

That was the advice Ken Hall gave to Nick Pencis when he asked permission to propose to his daughter, Jen.

"It was right here," Nick says. "I went over to the porch where she was, and after I proposed I looked up and saw a tear in his eye. My first thought was, I just broke one of his rules."

Nick had pretty much called Tyler home. His father was an executive chef, which took Nick all over the world as a kid.

"I hung out in a lot of kitchens. I would also gravitate towards the bands that played at those places. I knew at an early age that I was going to be a musician."

J.D. Stanley

Nick became a drummer and played in various bands. His last group was a three-piece jazz outfit with guitar and organ. "We were on the road for four years. It took us to 46 states."

Nick loved the life, but it does take its toll. Back home in Tyler, he took a job managing Stanley's Famous, an old established joint since 1958.

"Mr. Stanley had been sick. His children had established careers, so they sold it in 2000. That guy recently sold it to us. We bought it with help from Ken, Jen's dad."

Before they met, Jen was a massage therapist, personal trainer, Pilates instructor—as well as a recovering vegetarian.

"I was in town visiting my parents on my way back east. My mom and her friends took me here."

Nick adds, "I was friendly with everyone at the table, so I discreetly asked a friend's mother, 'Who's that with you?' She just took me over to Jen and proclaimed, 'This is Nick. He thinks you're gorgeous!' That made us both very uncomfortable, but I did get her number and four months later, I was right over there proposing to her."

Nick and Jen understand the burden of tradition they acquired, but that has not prevented them from putting their own twist on the place. They now have musical acts on the weekends, all with the blessing of Mr. Stanley's daughter, Pam.

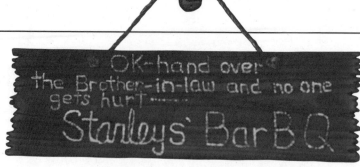

STANLEY'S FAMOUS
BROTHER-IN-LAW
HOT LINK,
BUTTERFLIED

Grill that bad boy on the flat side, then the round side. Toast a bun of your liking until lightly browned. Lay a piece of good ol' American cheese on the bottom bun and, in ascending order, place link, sauce, chopped beef brisket, sauce and top bun.

Barbecue pits and smokers are built many different ways with many different materials. This particular design is from Jack Easley of Marion Barbecue (see page 78–79. It appears in his booklet "Kentucky Bar-B-Q," which he sells at his place for $6 (tax included). It must be noted that a pit is merely a tool, like a saber saw. In a skilled operator's hands, beautiful results can be achieved. In the wrong, or untrained, hands, it just might cut off a hand.

MATERIALS

100 concrete blocks for pit and fireplace
(8 x 16 inch)

3 angle irons (52 inches long)

1 grill 46 x 54 inches (find this in a machine shop)

1 plywood board 64 x 72 x 1-inch

2 hinges for door

1 handle for door

2 (2 x 8-inch–5-feet-4-inch long) boards

2 (2 x 8-inch–6-foot long) boards

12 anchor bolts

1 thermometer (candy, jelly and deep-fry
thermometer, 200–400 degrees)

1 metal lintel, 32 inches long (to put over your fire
door to hold the last three layers of blocks)

1 piece of metal not less than 16 gauge, 28 x 20-
inch, to cover your firebox door

Fire bricks for firebox

Mortar mix

The foundation of your pit and fireplace should be 9-feet-4-inches long and 5-feet-4-inches wide. The concrete floor should be no less than 5 inches thick.

Build the firebox next to the pit for convenience. The firebox or fireplace will be 5 blocks high. Line the firebox with fire bricks. If you don't, the heat from the fire will break the blocks. It is not necessary to line the pit with fire brick because the pit will not get that hot.

The firebox will be open at the top and front.

The pit will also be 5 blocks high with a lid on top to hold in the heat and smoke. At the bottom of your pit there will be a fire door. The purpose of the fire door is to put the hot coals into the pit. These two doors will be the only openings to the pit.

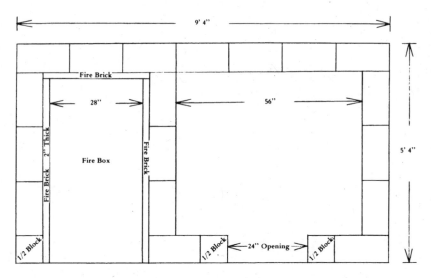

Fig. 1 Scale $^9/_{16}$ inch is 1 block

Step 1. This is your layer of blocks on the foundation. It will have 7 blocks across the back row. In your first layer of blocks you will only have 3 half-blocks and they are on the front. **See figure. 1.**

Step 2. Front of pit and top back of firebox. When you start your third layer of blocks put a metal lintel, 32 inches long over the fire door to hold the blocks. **See figure. 2.**

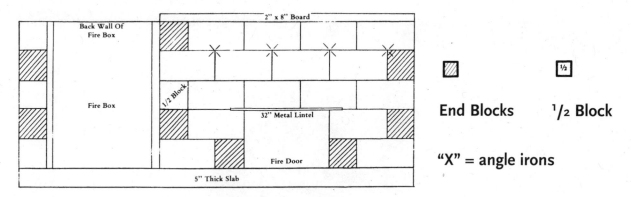

End Blocks   **$^1/_2$ Block**

"X" = angle irons

Fig. 2 Scale $^5/_8$ inch is 1 block

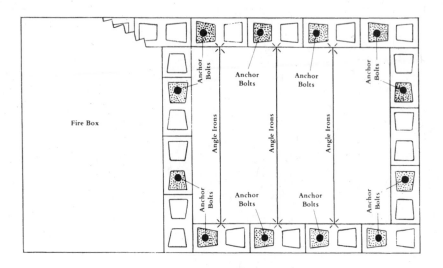

Fig. 3 Scale ⁵/₈ inch is 1 block

Step 3. When you finish the fourth round of blocks put the four angle irons (marked with x) across the pit. This is to hold the grill. **See figure. 3.**

Step 4. Add the fifth round of blocks. With the last layer of blocks put 12 anchor bolts in the blocks with cement. This will secure the 2 x 8-inch boards.

Step 5. Bolt down the 2 x 8-inch boards with nuts embedded into the board.

Step 6. Put the door on with hinges and a handle.

Step 7. Right in the center of your door, drill a small hole to put in the thermometer.

Step 8. Place a piece of metal not less than 16 gauge 28 x 20-inch to put in the front of the fire door. You can use a block to prop the metal up with. Whenever you need more air to the pit, just slide the metal over and let more air in.

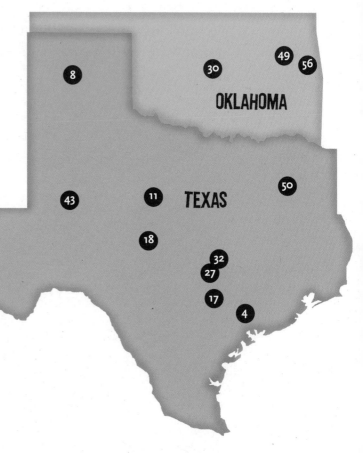

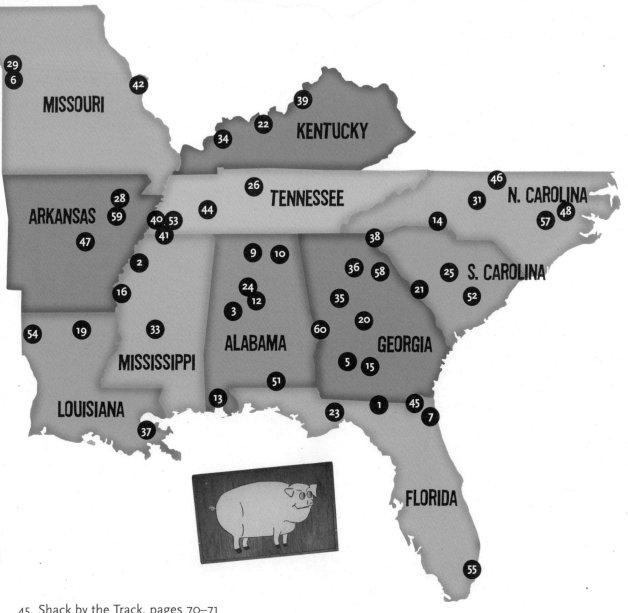

Recipe Index

People and Places Index